CONTENTS

DOMSIE

I

A LAD O' PAIRTS

The Revolution reached our parish years ago, and Drumtochty has a School Board, with a chairman and a clerk, besides a treasurer and an officer. Young Hillocks, who had two years in a lawyer's office, is clerk, and summons meetings by post, although he sees every member at the market or the kirk. Minutes are read with much solemnity, and motions to expend ten shillings upon a coal-cellar door passed, on the motion of Hillocks, seconded by Drumsheugh, who are both severely prompted for the occasion, and move uneasily before speaking.

Drumsheugh was at first greatly exalted by his poll, and referred freely on market days to his "plumpers," but as time went on the irony of the situation laid hold upon him.

"Think o' you and me, Hillocks, veesitin' the schule and sittin' wi' bukes in oor hands watchin' the Inspector. Keep's a', it's eneuch to mak' the auld Dominie turn in his grave. Twa meenisters cam' in his time, and Domsie put Geordie Hoo or some ither gleg laddie, that was makin' for college, thro' his facin's, and maybe some bit lassie brocht her copybuke. Syne they had their dinner, and Domsie tae, wi' the Doctor. Man, a've often thocht it was the prospeck o' the Schule Board and its weary bit rules that feenished Domsie. He wasna maybe sae shairp at the elements as this pirjinct body we hae noo, but a'body kent he was a terrible scholar and a credit tae the parish. Drumtochty was a name in thae days wi' the lads he sent tae college. It was maybe juist as weel he slippit awa' when he did, for he wud hae taen ill with thae new fikes, and nae college lad to warm his hert."

The present school-house stands in an open place beside the main road to Muirtown, treeless and comfortless, built of red, staring stone, with a play-ground for the boys and another for the girls, and a trim, smug-looking teacher's house, all very neat and symmetrical, and well regulated. The local paper had a paragraph headed "Drumtochty," written by the Muirtown architect, describing the whole premises in technical language that seemed to compensate the ratepayers for the cost, mentioning the contractor's name, and concluding that "this handsome building of the Scoto-Grecian style was one of the finest works that had ever come from the accomplished architect's hands." It has pitch-pine benches and map-cases, and a thermometer to be kept at not less than 58° and not more than 62°, and ventilators which the Inspector is careful to examine. When I stumbled in last week the teacher was drilling the children in Tonic Sol-fa with a little harmonium, and I left on tiptoe.

It is difficult to live up to this kind of thing, and my thoughts drift to the auld schule-house and Domsie. Some one with the love of God in his heart had built it long ago, and chose a site for the bairns in the sweet pine-woods at the foot of the cart road to Whinnie Knowe and the upland farms. It stood in a clearing with the tall Scotch firs round three sides, and on the fourth a brake of gorse and bramble bushes, through which there was an opening to the road. The clearing was the playground, and in summer the bairns annexed as much wood as they liked, playing tig among the trees, or sitting down at dinner-time on the soft, dry spines that made an elastic carpet everywhere. Domsie used to say there were two pleasant sights for his old eyes every day. One was to stand in the open at dinner-time and see the flitting forms of the healthy, rosy sonsie bairns in the wood, and from the door in the afternoon to watch the schule skail till each group was lost in the kindly shadow, and the merry shouts died away in this quiet place. Then the Dominie took a pinch of snuff and locked the door, and went to his house beside the school. One evening I came on him listening bare-headed to the voices, and he showed so kindly that I shall take him as he stands. A man of middle height, but stooping below it, with sandy hair turning to grey, and bushy eye-brow covering keen, shrewd grey eyes. You will notice that his linen is coarse but spotless, and that, though his clothes are worn almost threadbare, they are well brushed and orderly. But you will be chiefly arrested by the Dominie's coat, for the like of it was not in the parish. It was a black dress coat, and no man knew when it had begun its history; in its origin and its continuance it resembled Melchisedek. Many were the myths that gathered round that coat, but on this all were agreed, that without it we could not have realised the Dominie, and it became to us the sign and trappings of learning. He had taken a high place at the University, and won a good degree, and I've heard the Doctor say that he had a career before him. But something happened in his life, and Domsie buried himself among the woods with the bairns of Drumtochty. No one knew the story, but after he died I found a locket on his breast, with a proud, beautiful face within, and I have fancied it was a tragedy. It may have been in substitution that he gave all his love to the children, and nearly all his money too, helping lads to college, and affording an inexhaustible store of peppermints for the little ones.

Perhaps one ought to have been ashamed of that school-house, but yet it had its own distinction, for scholars were born there, and now and then to this day some famous man will come and stand in the deserted playground for a space. The door was at one end, and stood open in summer, so that the boys saw the rabbits come out from their holes on the edge of the wood, and birds sometimes flew in unheeded. The fireplace was at the other end, and was fed in winter with the sticks and peats brought by the scholars. On one side Domsie sat with the half-dozen lads he hoped to send to college, to whom he grudged no labour, and on the other gathered the very little ones, who used to warm their bare feet at the fire, while down the sides of the room the other scholars sat at their rough old desks, working sums and copying. Now and then a class came up and did some task, and at times a boy got the tawse for his negligence, but never a girl. He kept the girls in as their punishment, with a brother to take them home, and both had tea in Domsie's house, with a bit of his best honey, departing much torn between an honest wish to please Domsie and a pardonable longing for another tea.

"Domsie," as we called the schoolmaster, behind his back in Drumtochty, because we loved him, was true to the tradition of his kind, and had an unerring scent for "pairts" in his laddies. He could detect a scholar in the egg, and prophesied Latinity from a boy that seemed fit only to be a cowherd. It was believed that he had never made a mistake in judgment, and it was not his blame if the embryo scholar did not come to birth. "Five and thirty years have I been minister at Drumtochty," the Doctor used to say at school examinations, "and we have never wanted a student at the University, and while Dominie Jamieson lives we never shall." Whereupon Domsie took snuff, and assigned his share of credit to the Doctor, "who gave the finish in Greek to every lad of them, without money and without price, to make no mention of the higher mathematics." Seven ministers, four school-masters, four doctors, one professor, and three civil service men had been sent out by the auld schule in Domsie's time, besides many that "had given them-selves to mercantile pursuits."

He had a leaning to classics and the professions, but Domsie was catholic in his recognition of "pairts," and when the son of Hillocks' foreman made a collection of the insects of Drumtochty, there was a council at the manse. "Bumbee Willie," as he had been pleasantly called by his companions, was rescued from ridicule and encouraged to fulfil his bent. Once a year a long letter came to Mr. Patrick Jamieson, M.A., School-master, Drumtochty, N.B., and the address within was the British Museum. When Domsie read this letter to the school, he was always careful to explain that "Dr. Graham is the greatest living authority on beetles," and, generally speaking, if any clever lad did not care for Latin, he had the alternative of beetles.

But it was Latin Domsie hunted for as for fine gold, and when he found the smack of it in a lad he rejoiced openly. He counted it a day in his life when he knew certainly that he had hit on another scholar, and the whole school saw the identification of George Howe. For a winter Domsie had been "at point," racing George through Caesar, stalking him behind irregular verbs, baiting traps with tit-bits of Virgil. During these exercises Domsie surveyed George from above his spectacles with a hope that grew every day in assurance, and came to its height over a bit of Latin prose. Domsie tasted it visibly, and read it again in the shadow of the firs at meal-time, slapping his leg twice.

"He'll dae! he'll dae!" cried Domsie aloud, ladling in the snuff. "George, ma mannie, tell yir father that I am comin' up to Whinnie Knowe the nicht on a bit o' business."

Then the "schule" knew that Geordie Hoo was marked for college, and pelted him with fir cones in great gladness of heart.

"Whinnie" was full of curiosity over the Dominie's visit, and vexed Marget sorely, to whom Geordie had told wondrous things in the milk-house. "It canna be coals 'at he's wantin' frae the station, for there's a fell puckle left."

"And it'll no be seed taties," she said, pursuing the principle of exhaustion, "for he hes some Perthshire reds himsel'. I doot it's somethin' wrang with Geordie," and Whinnie started on a new track.

"He's been playin' truant maybe. A' mind gettin' ma paiks for birdnestin' masel. I'll wager that's the verra thing."

"Weel, yir wrang, Weelum," broke in Marget, Whinnie's wife, a tall, silent woman, with a speaking face; "it's naither the ae thing nor the ither, but something I've been prayin' for since Geordie was a wee bairn. Clean yirsel and meet Domsie on the road, for nae man deserves more honour in Drumtochty, naither laird nor farmer."

Conversation with us was a leisurely game, with slow movements and many pauses, and it was our custom to handle all the pawns before we brought the queen into action.

Domsie and Whinnie discussed the weather with much detail before they came in sight of George, but it was clear that Domsie was charged with something weighty, and even Whinnie felt that his own treatment of the turnip crop was wanting in repose.

At last Domsie cleared his throat and looked at Marget, who had been in and out, but ever within hearing.

"George is a fine laddie, Mrs. Howe."

An ordinary Drumtochty mother, although bursting with pride, would have responded, "He's weel eneuch, if he hed grace in his heart," in a tone that implied it was extremely unlikely, and that her laddie led the reprobates of the parish. As it was, Marget's face lightened, and she waited.

"What do you think of making him?" and the Dominie dropped the words slowly, for this was a moment in Drumtochty.

There was just a single ambition in those humble

homes, to have one of its members at college, and if Domsie approved a lad, then his brothers and sisters would give their wages, and the family would live on skim milk and oat cake, to let him have his chance.

Whinnie glanced at his wife and turned to Domsie.

"Marget's set on seein' Geordie a minister, Dominie."

"If he's worthy o't, no otherwise. We haena the means though; the farm is highly rented, and there's barely a penny over at the end o' the year."

"But you are willing George should go and see what he can do. If he disappoint you, then I dinna know a lad o' pairts when I see him, and the Doctor is with me."

"Maister Jamieson," said Marget, with great solemnity, "ma hert's desire is to see George a minister, and if the Almichty spared me to hear ma only bairn open his mooth in the Evangel, I wud hae naething mair to ask ... but I doot sair it canna be managed."

Domsie had got all he asked, and he rose in his strength.

"If George Howe disna get to college, then he's the first scholar I've lost in Drumtochty ... ye 'ill manage his keep and sic like?"

"Nae fear o' that," for Whinnie was warming, "tho' I haena a steek (stitch) o' new claithes for four years. But what aboot his fees and ither ootgaeins?"

"There's ae man in the parish can pay George's fees without missing a penny, and I'll warrant he 'ill dae it."

"Are ye meanin' Drumsheugh?" said Whinnie, "for ye 'ill never get a penny piece oot o' him. Did ye no hear hoo the Frees wiled him intae their kirk, Sabbath past a week, when Netherton's sister's son frae Edinboro' wes preaching the missionary sermon, expectin' a note, and if he didna change a shillin' at the public-hoose and pit in a penny. Sall, he's a lad Drumsheugh; a'm thinking ye may save yir journey, Dominie."

But Marget looked away from her into the past, and her eyes had a tender light. "He hed the best hert in the pairish aince."

Domsie found Drumsheugh inclined for company, and assisted at an exhaustive and caustic treatment of local affairs. When the conduct of Piggie Walker, who bought Drumsheugh's potatoes and went into bankruptcy without paying for a single tuber, had been characterized in language that left nothing to be desired, Drumsheugh began to soften and show signs of reciprocity.

"Hoo's yir laddies, Dominie?" whom the farmers regarded as a risky turnip crop in a stiff clay that Domsie had "to fecht awa in." "Are ony o' them shaping weel?"

Drumsheugh had given himself away, and Domsie laid his first parallel with a glowing account of George Howe's Latinity, which was well received.

"Weel, I'm gled tae hear sic accoonts o' Marget Hoo's son; there's naething in Whinnie but what the spune puts in."

But at the next move Drumsheugh scented danger and

stood at guard. "Na, na, Dominie, I see what yir aifter fine; ye mind hoo ye got three notes oot o' me at Perth market Martinmas a year past for ane o' yir college laddies. Five punds for four years; my word, yir no blate (modest). And what for sud I educat Marget Hoo's bairn? If ye kent a' ye wudna ask me; it's no reasonable, Dominie. So there's an end o't."

Domsie was only a pedantic old parish schoolmaster, and he knew little beyond his craft, but the spirit of the Humanists awoke within him, and he smote with all his might, bidding goodbye to his English as one flings away the scabbard of a sword.

"Ye think that a'm asking a great thing when I plead for a pickle notes to give a puir laddie a college education. I tell ye, man, a'm honourin' ye and givin' ye the fairest chance ye'll ever hae o' winning wealth. Gin ye store the money ye hae scrapit by mony a hard bargain, some heir ye never saw 'ill gar it flee in chambering and wantonness. Gin ye hed the heart to spend it on a lad o' pairts like Geordie Hoo, ye wud hae twa rewards nae man could tak fra ye. Ane wud be the honest gratitude o' a laddie whose desire for knowledge ye hed sateesfied, and the second wud be this - anither scholar in the land; and a'm thinking with auld John Knox that ilka scholar is something added to the riches of the commonwealth. And what 'ill it cost ye? Little mair than the price o' a cattle beast. Man, Drumsheugh, ye poverty-stricken cratur, I've naethin' in this world but a handfu' o' books and a ten-pund note for my funeral, and yet, if it wasna I have all my brither's bairns tae keep, I wud pay every penny mysel'. But I'll no see Geordie sent to the plough, tho' I gang frae door to door. Na, na, the grass 'ill no grow on the road atween the college and the schule-hoose o'

Drumtochty till they lay me in the auld kirkyard."

"Sall, Domsie was roosed," Drumsheugh explained in the Muirtown inn next market. "'Miserly wratch' was the ceevilest word on his tongue. He wud naither sit nor taste, and was half way doon the yaird afore I cud quiet him. An' a'm no sayin' he hed na reason if I'd been meanin' a' I said. It wud be a scan'al to the pairish if a likely lad cudna win tae college for the want o' siller. Na, na, neeburs, we hae oor faults, but we're no sae dune mean as that in Drumtochty."

As it was, when Domsie did depart he could only grip Drumsheugh's hand, and say Maecenas, and was so intoxicated, but not with strong drink, that he explained to Hillocks on the way home that Drumsheugh would be a credit to Drumtochty, and that his Latin style reminded him of Cicero. He added as an afterthought that Whinnie Knowe had promised to pay Drumsheugh's fees for four years at the University of Edinburgh.

II

HOW WE CARRIED THE NEWS
TO WHINNIE KNOWE

Domsie was an artist, and prepared the way for George's University achievement with much cunning. Once every Sabbath in the kirk-yard, where he laid down the law beneath an old elm tree, and twice between Sabbaths, at the post-office and by the wayside, he adjured us not to expect beyond measure, and gave us reasons.

"Ye see, he has a natural talent for learning, and took to Latin like a duck to water. What could be done in Drumtochty was done for him, and he's working night and day, but he'll have a sore fight with the lads from the town schools. Na, na, neighbours," said the Dominie, lapsing into dialect, "we daurna luik for a prize. No the first year, at ony rate."

"Man, Dominie. A'm clean astonished at ye," Drumsheugh used to break in, who, since he had given to George's support, outran us all in his faith, and had no patience with Domsie's devices, "a' tell ye if Geordie disna get a first in every class he's entered for, the judges 'ill be a puir lot," with a fine confusion of circumstances.

"Losh, Drumsheugh, be quiet, or ye'll dae the laddie an injury," said Domsie, with genuine alarm. "We maunna mention prizes, and first is fair madness, A certificate of honour now, that will be aboot it, may be next to the prizemen."

Coming home from market he might open his heart. "George 'ill be amang the first sax, or my name is no Jamieson," but generally he prophesied a moderate success. There were times when he affected indifference, and talked cattle. We then regarded him with awe, because this was more than mortal.

It was my luck to carry the bulletin to Domsie, and I learned what he had been enduring. It was good manners in Drumtochty to feign amazement at the sight of a letter, and to insist that it must be intended for some other person. When it was finally forced upon one, you examined the handwriting at various angles and speculated about the writer. Some felt emboldened, after these precautions, to open the letter, but this haste was considered indecent. When Posty handed Drumsheugh the factor's letter, with the answer to his offer for the farm, he only remarked, "It'll be frae the factor," and harked back to a polled Angus bull he had seen at the show. "Sall," said Posty in the kirkyard with keen relish, "ye'll never flurry Drumsheugh." Ordinary letters were read in leisurely retirement, and, in case of urgency, answered within the week.

Domsie clutched the letter, and would have torn off the envelope. But he could not; his hand was shaking like an aspen. He could only look, and I read:

"Dear Mr. Jamieson, - The class honour lists are just out, and you will be pleased to know that I have got the medal both in the Humanity and the Greek."

There was something about telling his mother, and his gratitude to his schoolmaster, but Domsie heard no more. He tried to speak and could not, for a rain of tears was on his hard old face. Domsie was far more a pagan than a saint, but somehow he seemed to me that day as Simeon, who had at last seen his heart's desire, and was satisfied.

When the school had dispersed with a joyful shout, and disappeared in the pine woods, he said, "Ye'll come too," and I knew he was going to Whinnie Knowe. He did not speak one word upon the way, but twice he stood and read the letter which he held fast in his hand. His face was set as he climbed the cart track. I saw it set again as we came down that road one day, but it was well that we could not pierce beyond the present.

Whinnie left his plough in the furrow, and came to meet us, taking two drills at a stride, and shouting remarks on the weather yards off.

Domsie only lifted the letter. "Frae George."

"Ay, ay, and what's he gotten noo?"

Domsie solemnly unfolded the letter, and brought down his spectacles. "Edinburgh, April 7th." Then he looked at Whinnie, and closed his mouth.

"We'll tell it first to his mither."

"Yer richt, Dominie. She weel deserves it. A'm thinking she's seen us by this time." So we fell into a procession, Dominie leading by two yards; and then a

Ian Maclaren

strange thing happened. For the first and last time in his life Domsie whistled, and the tune was "A hundred pipers and a' and a'," and as he whistled he seemed to dilate before our eyes, and he struck down thistles with his stick - a thistle at every stroke.

"Domsie's fair carried," whispered Whinnie, "it cowes a'."

Marget met us at the end of the house beside the brier bush, where George was to sit on summer afternoons before he died, and a flash passed between Domsie and the lad's mother. Then she knew that it was well, and fixed her eyes on the letter, but Whinnie, his thumbs in his armholes, watched the wife.

Domsie now essayed to read the news, but between the shaking of his hands and his voice he could not.

"It's nae use," he cried, "he's first in the Humanity oot o' a hundred and seeventy lads, first o' them a', and he's first in the Greek too; the like o' this is hardly known, and it has na been seen in Drumtochty since there was a schule. That's the word he's sent, and he bade me tell his mother without delay, and I am here as fast as my old feet could carry me."

I glanced round, although I did not myself see very clearly.

Marget was silent for the space of five seconds; she was a good woman, and I knew that better afterwards. She took the Dominie's hand, and said to him, "Under God this was your doing, Maister Jamieson, and for your reward ye'ill get naither silver nor gold, but ye hae a mither's gratitude."

Whinnie gave a hoarse chuckle and said to his wife, "It was frae you, Marget, he got it a'."

When we settled in the parlour Domsie's tongue was loosed, and he lifted up his voice and sang the victory of Geordie Hoo.

"It's ten years ago at the brak up o' the winter ye brought him down to me, Mrs. Hoo, and ye said at the schule-hoose door, 'Dinna be hard on him, Maister Jamieson, he's my only bairn, and a wee thingie quiet.' Div ye mind what I said, 'There's something ahint that face,' and my heart warmed to George that hour. Two years after the Doctor examined the schule, and he looks at George. 'That's a likely lad, Dominie. What think ye?' And he was only eight years auld, and no big for his size. 'Doctor, I daurna prophesy till we turn him into the Latin, but a've my thoughts.' So I had a' the time, but I never boasted, na, na, that's dangerous. Didna I say, 'Ye hev a promisin' laddie, Whinnie,' ae day in the market?"

"It's a fac'," said Whinnie, "it wes the day I bocht the white coo." But Domsie swept on.

"The first year o' Latin was enough for me. He juist nippet up his verbs. Cæsar could na keep him going; he wes into Virgil afore he wes eleven, and the Latin prose, man, as sure as a'm living, it tasted o' Cicero frae the beginning."

Whinnie wagged his head in amazement.

"It was the verra nicht o' the Latin prose I cam up to speak aboot the college, and ye thocht Geordie hed been playing truant."

Ian Maclaren

Whinnie laughed uproariously, but Domsie heeded not.

"It was awfu' work the next twa years, but the Doctor stood in weel wi' the Greek. Ye mind hoo Geordie tramped ower the muir to the manse thro' the weet an' the snaw, and there wes aye dry stockings for him in the kitchen afore he had his Greek in the Doctor's study."

"And a warm drink tae," put in Marget, "and that's the window I pit the licht in to guide him hame in the dark winter nichts, and mony a time when the sleet played swish on the glass I wes near wishin' - " Domsie waved his hand.

"But that's dune wi' noo, and he was worth a' the toil and trouble. First in the Humanity and first in the Greek, sweepit the field, Lord preserve us. A' can hardly believe it. Eh, I was feared o' thae High School lads. They had terrible advantages. Maisters frae England, and tutors, and whatna', but Drumtochty carried aff the croon. It'll be fine reading in the papers -

Humanity. - First Prize (and Medal), George Howe, Drumtochty, Perthshire.

Greek. - First Prize (and Medal), George Howe, Drumtochty, Perthshire."

"It'll be michty," cried Whinnie, now fairly on fire.

"And Philosophy and Mathematics to come. Geordie's no bad at Euclid, I'll wager he'll be first there too. When he gets his hand in there's naething he's no fit for wi' time. My ain laddie - and the Doctor's - we maunna forget him - it's his classics he hes, every book o' them.

The Doctor 'ill be lifted when he comes back on Saturday. A'm thinkin' we'll hear o't on Sabbath. And Drumsheugh, he'll be naither to had nor bind in the kirk-yard. As for me, I wad na change places wi' the Duke o' Athole," and Domsie shook the table to its foundation.

Then he awoke, as from a dream, and the shame of boasting that shuts the mouths of self-respecting Scots descended upon him.

"But this is fair nonsense. Ye'll no mind the havers o' an auld dominie."

He fell back on a recent roup, and would not again break away, although sorely tempted by certain of Whinnie's speculations.

When I saw him last, his coat-tails were waving victoriously as he leaped a dyke on his way to tell our Drumtochty Maecenas that the judges knew their business.

III

IN MARGET'S GARDEN

The cart track to Whinnie Knowe was commanded by a gable window, and Whinnie boasted that Marget had never been taken unawares. Tramps, finding every door locked, and no sign of life anywhere, used to express their mind in the "close," and return by the way they came, while ladies from Kildrummie, fearful lest they should put Mrs. Howe out, were met at the garden gate by Marget in her Sabbath dress, and brought into a set tea as if they had been invited weeks before.

Whinnie gloried most in the discomfiture of the Tory agent, who had vainly hoped to coerce him in the stack yard without Marget's presence, as her intellectual contempt for the Conservative party knew no bounds.

"Sall she saw him slip aff the road afore the last stile, and wheep roond the fit o' the gairden wa' like a tod (fox) aifter the chickens.

"'It's a het day, Maister Anderson,' says Marget frae the gairden, lookin' doon on him as calm as ye like. 'Yir surely no gaein' to pass oor hoose without a gless o' milk?'

"Wud ye believe it, he wes that upset he left withoot sayin' 'vote,' and Drumsheugh telt me next market that his langidge aifterwards cudna be printed."

When George came home for the last time, Marget went back and forward all afternoon from his bedroom to the window, and hid herself beneath the laburnum to see his face as the cart stood before the stile. It told her plain what she had feared, and Marget passed through her Gethsemane with the gold blossoms falling on her face. When their eyes met, and before she helped him down, mother and son understood.

"Ye mind what I told ye, o' the Greek mothers, the day I left. Weel, I wud hae liked to have carried my shield, but it wasna to be, so I've come home on it." As they went slowly up the garden walk, "I've got my degree, a double first, mathematics and classics."

"Ye've been a gude soldier, George, and faithfu'."

"Unto death, a'm dootin, mother."

"Na," said Marget, "unto life."

Drumtochty was not a heartening place in sickness, and Marget, who did not think our thoughts, endured much consolation at her neighbour's hands. It is said that in cities visitors congratulate a patient on his good looks, and deluge his family with instances of recovery. This would have seemed to us shallow and unfeeling, besides being a "temptin' o' Providence," which might not have intended to go to extremities, but on a challenge of this kind had no alternative. Sickness was regarded as a distinction tempered with judgment, and favoured people found it difficult to be humble. I always thought more of Peter MacIntosh when the mysterious "tribble" that needed the Perth doctor made no difference in his manner, and he passed his snuff box across the seat before the long prayer as usual, but in this indifference to privileges Peter was exceptional.

You could never meet Kirsty Stewart on equal terms, although she was quite affable to any one who knew his place.

"Ay," she said, on my respectful allusion to her experience, "a've seen mair than most. It doesna become me to boast, but tho' I say it as sudna, I hae buried a' my ain fouk."

Kirsty had a "way" in sick visiting, consisting in a certain cadence of the voice and arrangement of the face, which was felt to be soothing and complimentary.

"Yir aboot again, a'm glad to see," to me after my accident, "but yir no dune wi' that leg; na, na, Jeems, that was ma second son, scrapit his shin aince, tho' no so bad as ye've dune a'm hearing (for I had denied Kirsty the courtesy of an inspection). It's sax year syne noo, and he got up and wes traivellin' fell hearty like yersel. But he begood to dwam (sicken) in the end of the year, and soughed awa' in the spring. Ay, ay, when tribble comes ye never ken hoo it 'ill end. A' thocht I wud come up and speir for ye. A body needs comfort gin he's sober (ill)."

When I found George wrapped in his plaid beside the brier bush whose roses were no whiter than his cheeks, Kirsty was already installed as comforter in the parlour, and her drone came through the open window.

"Ay, ay, Marget, sae it's come to this. Weel, we daurna complain, ye ken. Be thankfu' ye haena lost your man and five sons, besides twa sisters and a brither, no to mention cousins. That wud be something to speak aboot, and Losh keep's, there's nae saying but he micht hang on a whilie. Ay, ay, it's a sair blow aifter a' that wes in the papers. I wes feared when I heard o' the papers; 'Lat weel alane,' says I to the Dominie; 'ye 'ill bring a judgment on the laddie wi' yir blawing.' But ye micht as weel hae spoken to the hills. Domsie's a thraun body at the best, and he was clean infatuat' wi' George. Ay, ay, it's an awfu' lesson, Marget, no to mak' idols o' our bairns, for that's naethin' else than provokin' the Almichty."

It was at this point that Marget gave way and scandalized Drumtochty, which held that obtrusive prosperity was an irresistible provocation to the higher powers, and that a skilful depreciation of our children was a policy of safety.

"Did ye say the Almichty? I'm thinkin' that's ower grand a name for your God, Kirsty. What wud ye think o' a faither that brocht hame some bonnie thing frae the fair for ane o' his bairns, and when the puir bairn wes pleased wi' it tore it oot o' his hand and flung it into the fire? Eh, woman, he wud be a meeserable cankered jealous body. Kirsty, wumman, when the Almichty sees a mither bound up in her laddie, I tell ye He is sair pleased in His heaven, for mind ye hoo He loved His ain Son. Besides, a'm judgin' that nane o' us can love anither withoot lovin' Him, or hurt anither withoot hurtin' Him.

"Oh, I ken weel that George is gaein' to leave us; but it's no because the Almichty is jealous o' him or me, no

Ian Maclaren

likely. It cam' to me last nicht that He needs my laddie for some grand wark in the ither world, and that's hoo George has his bukes brocht oot tae the garden and studies a' the day. He wants to be ready for his kingdom, just as he trachled in the bit schule o' Drumtochty for Edinboro'. I hoped he wud hae been a minister o' Christ's Gospel here, but he 'ill be judge over many cities yonder. A'm no denyin', Kirsty, that it's a trial, but I hae licht on it, and naethin' but gude thochts o' the Almichty."

Drumtochty understood that Kirsty had dealt faithfully with Marget for pride and presumption, but all we heard was, "Losh keep us a'."

When Marget came out and sat down beside her son, her face was shining. Then she saw the open window.

"I didna ken."

"Never mind, mither, there's nae secrets atween us, and it gar'd my heart leap to hear ye speak up like yon for God, and to know yir content. Div ye mind the nicht I called for ye, mother, and ye gave me the Gospel aboot God?"

Marget slipped her hand into George's, and he let his head rest on her shoulder. The likeness flashed upon me in that moment, the earnest deep-set grey eyes, the clean-cut firm jaw, and the tender mobile lips, that blend of apparent austerity and underlying romance that make the pathos of a Scottish face.

"There had been a Revival man, here," George explained to me, "and he was preaching on hell. As it grew dark a candle was lighted, and I can still see his face as in a picture, a hard-visaged man. He looked down at us laddies in the front, and asked us if we knew what like hell was. By this time we were that terrified none of us could speak, but I whispered 'No.'

"Then he rolled up a piece of paper and held it in the flame, and we saw it burn and glow and shrivel up and fall in black dust.

"'Think,' said he, and he leaned over the desk, and spoke in a gruesome whisper which made the cold run down our backs, 'that yon paper was your finger, one finger only of your hand, and it burned like that for ever and ever, and think of your hand and your arm and your whole body all on fire, never to go out.' We shuddered that you might have heard the form creak. 'That is hell, and that is where ony laddie will go who does not repent and believe.'

"It was like Dante's Inferno, and I dared not take my eyes off his face. He blew out the candle, and we crept to the door trembling, not able to say one word.

"That night I could not sleep, for I thought I might be in the fire before morning. It was harvest time, and the moon was filling the room with cold clear light. From my bed I could see the stooks standing in rows upon the field, and it seemed like the judgment day.

"I was only a wee laddie, and I did what we all do in trouble, I cried for my mother.

"Ye hae na forgotten, mither, the fricht that was on me that nicht."

" Never, " said Marget, "and never can; it's hard wark

Ian Maclaren

for me to keep frae hating that man, dead or alive. Geordie gripped me wi' baith his wee airms round my neck, and he cries over and over and over again, 'Is yon God?'"

"Ay, and ye kissed me, mither, and ye said (it's like yesterday), 'Yir safe with me,' and ye telt me that God micht punish me to mak me better if I was bad, but that he wud never torture ony puir soul, for that cud dae nae guid, and was the Devil's wark. Ye asked me:

"'Am I a guid mother tae ye?' and when I could dae naethin' but hold, ye said, 'Be sure God maun be a hantle kinder.'

"The truth came to me as with a flicker, and I cuddled down into my bed, and fell asleep in His love as in my mother's arms.

"Mither," and George lifted up his head, "that was my conversion, and, mither dear, I hae longed a' thro' thae college studies for the day when ma mooth wud be opened wi' this evangel."

Marget's was an old-fashioned garden, with pinks and daisies and forget-me-nots, with sweet-scented wall-flower and thyme and moss roses, where nature had her way, and gracious thoughts could visit one without any jarring note. As George's voice softened to the close, I caught her saying, "His servants shall see His face," and the peace of Paradise fell upon us in the shadow of death.

The night before the end George was carried out to his corner, and Domsie, whose heart was nigh unto the breaking, sat with him the afternoon. They used to fight the College battles over again, with their favourite classics beside them, but this time none of them spoke of books. Marget was moving about the garden, and she told me that George looked at Domsie wistfully, as if he had something to say and knew not how to do it.

After a while he took a book from below his pillow, and began, like one thinking over his words:

"Maister Jamieson, ye hae been a gude freend tae me, the best I ever hed aifter my mither and faither. Wull ye tak this buik for a keepsake o' yir grateful scholar? It's a Latin 'Imitation' Dominie, and it's bonnie printin'. Ye mind hoo ye gave me yir ain Virgil, and said he was a kind o' Pagan sanct. Noo here is my sanct, and div ye ken I've often thocht Virgil saw His day afar off, and was glad. Wull ye read it, Dominie, for my sake, and maybe ye 'ill come to see - " and George could not find words for more.

But Domsie understood. "Ma laddie, ma laddie, that I luve better than onythin' on earth, I'll read it till I die, and, George, I'll tell ye what livin' man does na ken. When I was your verra age I had a cruel trial, and ma heart was turned frae faith. The classics hae been my bible, though I said naethin' to ony man against Christ. He aye seemed beyond man, and noo the veesion o' Him has come to me in this gairden. Laddie, ye hae dune far mair for me than I ever did for you. Wull ye mak a prayer for yir auld dominie afore we pairt?"

There was a thrush singing in the birches and a sound of bees in the air, when George prayed in a low, soft voice, with a little break in it.

"Lord Jesus, remember my dear maister, for he's been a kind freend to me and mony a puir laddie in Drumtochty. Bind up his sair heart and give him licht at eventide, and may the maister and his scholars meet some mornin' where the schule never skails, in the kingdom o' oor Father."

Twice Domsie said Amen, and it seemed as the voice of another man, and then he kissed George upon the forehead; but what they said Marget did not wish to hear.

When he passed out at the garden gate, the westering sun was shining golden, and the face of Domsie was like unto that of a little child.

IV

A SCHOLAR'S FUNERAL

Drumtochty never acquitted itself with credit at a marriage, having no natural aptitude for gaiety, and being haunted with anxiety lest any "hicht" should end in a "howe," but the parish had a genius for funerals. It was long mentioned with a just sense of merit that an English undertaker, chancing on a "beerial" with us, had no limits to his admiration. He had been disheartened to despair all his life by the ghastly efforts of chirpy little Southerners to look solemn on occasion, but his dreams were satisfied at the sight of men like Drumsheugh and Hillocks in their Sabbath blacks. Nature lent an initial advantage in face, but it was an instinct in the blood that brought our manner to perfection, and nothing could be more awful than a group of those austere figures, each man gazing into vacancy without a trace of expression, and refusing to recognise his nearest neighbour by word or look. Drumtochty gave itself to a "beerial" with chastened satisfaction, partly because it lay near to the sorrow of things, and partly because there was nothing of speculation in it. "Ye can hae little rael pleesure in a merrige," explained our gravedigger, in whom the serious side had been perhaps abnormally developed, "for ye never ken hoo it will end; but there's nae risk about a 'beerial.'"

Ian Maclaren

It came with a shock upon townsmen that the ceremony began with a "service o' speerits," and that an attempt of the Free Kirk minister to replace this by the reading of Scripture was resisted as an "innovation." Yet every one admitted that the seriousness of Drumtochty pervaded and sanctified this function. A tray of glasses was placed on a table with great solemnity by the "wricht," who made no sign and invited none. You might have supposed that the circumstance had escaped the notice of the company, so abstracted and unconscious was their manner, had it not been that two graven images a minute later are standing at the table.

"Ye 'ill taste, Tammas," with settled melancholy.

"Na, na; I've nae incleenation the day; it's an awfu' dispensation this, Jeems. She wud be barely saxty."

"Ay, ay, but we maun keep up the body sae lang as we're here, Tammas."

"Weel, puttin' it that way, a'm not sayin' but yir richt," yielding unwillingly to the force of circumstance.

"We're here the day and there the morn, Tammas. She wes a fine wumman - Mistress Stirton - a weel-livin' wumman; this 'ill be a blend, a'm thinkin'."

"She slippit aff sudden in the end; a'm judgin' it's frae the Muirtown grocer; but a body canna discreeminate on a day like this."

Before the glasses are empty all idea of drinking is dissipated, and one has a vague impression that he is at church.

It was George Howe's funeral that broke the custom and closed the "service." When I came into the garden where the neighbours were gathered, the "wricht" was removing his tray, and not a glass had been touched. Then I knew that Drumtochty had a sense of the fitness of things, and was stirred to its depths.

"Ye saw the wricht carry in his tray," said Drumsheugh, as we went home from the kirkyard. "Weel, yon's the last sicht o't ye 'ill get, or a'm no Drumsheugh. I've nae objection ma'sel to a nee'bur tastin' at a funeral, a' the mair if he's come frae the upper end o' the pairish, and ye ken I dinna hold wi' thae teetotal fouk. A'm ower auld in the horn to change noo. But there's times and seasons, as the gude Buik says, and it wud hae been an awfu' like business tae luik at a gless in Marget's gairden, and puir Domsie standing in ahent the brier bush as if he cud never lift his heid again. Ye may get shairper fouk in the uptak', but ye 'ill no get a pairish with better feelin's. It 'ill be a kind o' sateesfaction tae Marget when she hears o't. She was aye against tastin', and a'm judgin' her tribble has ended it at beerials."

"Man, it was hard on some o' yon lads the day, but there wesna ane o' them made a mudge. I keepit my eye on Posty, but he never lookit the way it wes. He's a drouthy body, but he hes his feelin's, hes Posty."

Before the Doctor began the prayer, Whinnie took me up to the room.

"There's twa o' Geordie's College freends with Marget, grand scholars a'm telt, and there's anither I canna weel mak oot. He's terrible cast doon, and Marget speaks as if she kent him."

It was a low-roofed room, with a box bed and some pieces of humble furniture, fit only for a labouring man. But the choice treasures of Greece and Rome lay on the table, and on a shelf beside the bed College prizes and medals, while everywhere were the roses he loved. His peasant mother stood beside the body of her scholar son, whose hopes and thoughts she had shared, and through the window came the bleating of distant sheep. It was the idyll of Scottish University life.

George's friends were characteristic men, each of his own type, and could only have met in the common-wealth of letters. One was of an ancient Scottish house which had fought for Mary against the Lords of the Congregation, followed Prince Charlie to Culloden, and were High Church and Tory to the last drop of their blood. Ludovic Gordon left Harrow with the reputation of a classic, and had expected to be first at Edinboro'. It was Gordon, in fact, that Domsie feared in the great war, but he proved second to Marget's son, and being of the breed of Prince Jonathan, which is the same the world over, he came to love our David as his own soul. The other, a dark little man, with a quick, fiery eye, was a Western Celt, who had worried his way from a fishing croft in Barra to be an easy first in Philosophy at Edinboro', and George and Ronald Maclean were as brothers because there is nothing so different as Scottish and Highland blood.

"Maister Gordon," said Marget, "this is George's Homer, and he bade me tell you that he coonted yir freendship ain o' the gifts o' God."

For a brief space Gordon was silent, and, when he spoke, his voice sounded strange in that room.

"Your son was the finest scholar of my time, and a very perfect gentleman. He was also my true friend, and I pray God to console his mother." And Ludovic Gordon bowed low over Marget's worn hand as if she had been a queen.

Marget lifted Plato, and it seemed to me that day as if the dignity of our Lady of Sorrows had fallen upon her.

"This is the buik George chose for you, Maister Maclean, for he aye said to me ye hed been a prophet and shown him mony deep things."

The tears sprang to the Celt's eyes.

"It wass like him to make all other men better than himself," with the soft, sad Highland accent; "and a proud woman you are to hef been his mother."

The third man waited at the window till the scholars left, and then I saw he was none of that kind, but one who had been a slave of sin and now was free.

"Andra Chaumers, George wished ye tae hev his Bible, and he expecks ye tae keep the tryst."

"God helping me, I will," said Chalmers, hoarsely; and from the garden ascended a voice, "O God, who art a very present help in trouble."

The Doctor's funeral prayer was one of the glories of the parish, compelling even the Free Kirk to reluctant admiration, although they hinted that its excellence was rather of the letter than the spirit, and regarded its indiscriminate charity with suspicion. It opened with a series of extracts from the Psalms, relieved by two excursions into the minor prophets, and led up to a sonorous recitation of the problem of immortality from Job, with its triumphant solution in the peroration of the fifteenth chapter of I Corinthians. Drumtochty men held their breath till the Doctor reached the crest of the hill (Hillocks disgraced himself once by dropping his staff at the very moment when the Doctor was passing from Job to Paul), and then we relaxed while the Doctor descended to local detail. It was understood that it took twenty years to bring the body of this prayer to perfection, and any change would have been detected and resented.

The Doctor made a good start, and had already sighted Job, when he was carried out of his course by a sudden current, and began to speak to God about Marget and her son, after a very simple fashion that brought a lump to the throat, till at last, as I imagine, the sight of the laddie working at his Greek in the study of a winter night came up before him, and the remnants of the great prayer melted like an iceberg in the Gulf Stream.

"Lord, hae peety upon us, for we a' luved him, and we were a' prood o' him."

After the Doctor said "Amen" with majesty, one used to look at his neighbour, and the other would shut his eyes and shake his head, meaning, "There's no use asking me, for it simply can't be better done by living man." This time no one remembered his neighbour, because every eye was fixed on the Doctor. Drumtochty was identifying its new minister.

"It may be that I hef judged him hardly," said Lachlan Campbell, one of the Free Kirk Highlanders, and our St. Dominic. "I shall never again deny that the root of the matter is in the man, although much choked with the tares of worldliness and Arminianism."

"He is a goot man, Lachlan," replied Donald Menzies, another Celt, and he was our St. Francis, for "every one that loveth is born of God."

There was no hearse in Drumtochty, and we carried our dead by relays of four, who waded every stream unless more than knee deep, the rest following in straggling, picturesque procession over the moor and across the stepping stones. Before we started, Marget came out and arranged George's white silken hood upon the coffin with roses in its folds.

She swept us into one brief flush of gratitude, from Domsie to Posty.

"Neeburs, ye were a' his freends, and he wanted ye tae ken hoo yir trust wes mickle help tae him in his battle."

There was a stir within us, and it came to birth in Drumsheugh of all men:

"Marget Hoo, this is no the day for mony words, but there's juist ae heart in Drumtochty, and it's sair."

No one spoke to Domsie as we went down the cart track, with the ripe corn standing on either side, but he beckoned Chalmers to walk with him.

"Ye hae heard him speak o' me, then, Maister Jamieson?"

"Ay, oftentimes, and he said once that ye were hard driven, but that ye had trampled Satan under yir feet."

"He didna tell ye all, for if it hadna been for George Howe I wudna been worth callin' a man this day. One night when he was workin' hard for his honours examination and his disease was heavy upon him, puir fellow, he sought me oot where I was, and wouldna leave till I cam' wi him.

"'Go home,' I said, 'Howe; it's death for ye to be oot in this sleet and cold. Why not leave me to lie in the bed I hae made?'

"He took me by the arm into a passage. I see the gaslicht on his white face, and the shining o' his eyes.

"'Because I have a mother...'

"Dominie, he pulled me oot o' hell."

"Me tae, Andra, but no your hell. Ye mind the Roman Triumph, when a general cam' hame wi' his spoils. Laddie, we're the captives that go with his chariot up the Capitol."

Donald Menzies was a man of moods, and the Doctor's prayer had loosed his imagination so that he saw visions.

"Look," said he, as we stood on a ridge, "I hef seen it before in the book of Joshua."

Below the bearers had crossed a burn on foot, and were ascending the slope where an open space of deep green was fringed with purple heather.

"The ark hass gone over Jordan, and George will have come into the Land of Promise."

The September sunshine glinted on the white silk George won with his blood, and fell like a benediction on the two figures that climbed the hard ascent close after the man they loved.

Strangers do not touch our dead in Drumtochty, but the eight of nearest blood lower the body into the grave. The order of precedence is keenly calculated, and the loss of a merited cord can never be forgiven. Marget had arranged everything with Whinnie, and all saw the fitness. His father took the head, and the feet (next in honour) he gave to Domsie.

"Ye maun dae it. Marget said ye were o' his ain bluid."

On the right side the cords were handed to the Doctor, Gordon, and myself; and on the left to Drumsheugh, Maclean, and Chalmers. Domsie lifted the hood for Marget, but the roses he gently placed on George's name. Then with bent, uncovered heads, and in unbroken silence, we buried all that remained of our scholar.

We always waited till the grave was filled and the turf laid down, a trying quarter of an hour. Ah me! the thud of the spade on your mother's grave! None gave any sign of what he felt save Drumsheugh, whose sordid slough had slipped off from a tender heart, and Chalmers, who went behind a tombstone and sobbed aloud. Not even Posty asked the reason so much as by a look, and Drumtochty, as it passed, made as though it did not see. But I marked that the Dominie took Chalmers home, and walked all the way with him to Kildrummie station next morning. His friends erected a granite cross over George's grave, and it was left to Domsie to choose the inscription. There was a day when it would have been "Whom the gods love die young." Since then Domsie had seen the kingdom of God, and this is graven where the roses bloomed fresh every summer for twenty years till Marget was laid with her son:

GEORGE HOWE, M.A., Died September 22nd, 1869, Aged 21.

"They shall bring the glory and honour of the nations into it."

It was a late November day when I went to see George's memorial, and the immortal hope was burning low in my heart; but as I stood before that cross, the sun struggled from behind a black watery bank of cloud, and picked out every letter of the Apocalypse in gold.

A HIGHLAND MYSTIC

I

WHAT EYE HATH NOT SEEN

Strange ministers who came to assist at the Free Kirk Sacrament were much impressed with the elders, and never forgot the transfiguration of Donald Menzies, which used to begin about the middle of the "action" sermon, and was completed at the singing of the last Psalm. Once there was no glory, because the minister, being still young, expounded a new theory of the atonement of German manufacture, and Donald's face was piteous to behold. It haunted the minister for months, and brought to confusion a promising course of sermons on the contribution of Hegel to Christian thought. Donald never laid the blame of such calamities on the preacher, but accepted them as a just judgment on his blindness of heart.

"We hef had the open vision," Donald explained to his friend Lachlan Campbell, who distributed the responsibility in another fashion, "and we would not see - so the veil hass fallen."

Donald sat before the pulpit and filled the hearts of nervous probationers with dismay, not because his face was critical, but because it seemed non-conducting, upon which their best passages would break like spray against a rock. It was by nature the dullest you ever saw, with hair descending low upon the forehead, and preposterous whiskers dominating everything that remained, except a heavy mouth and brown, lack-lustre eyes. For a while Donald crouched in the corner of the pew, his head sunk on his breast, a very picture of utter hopelessness. But as the Evangel began to play round his heart, he would fix the preacher with rapid, wistful glances, as of one who had awaked but hardly dared believe such things could be true. Suddenly a sigh pervaded six pews, a kind of gentle breath of penitence, faith, love, and hope mingled together like the incense of the sanctuary, and Donald lifted up his head. His eyes are now aflame, and those sullen lips are refining into curves of tenderness. From the manse pew I watched keenly, for at any moment a wonderful sight may be seen. A radiant smile will pass from his lips to his eyes and spread over his face, as when the sun shines on a fallow field and the rough furrows melt into warmth and beauty. Donald's gaze is now fixed on a window above the preacher's head, for on these great days that window is to him as the gate of heaven. All I could see would be a bit of blue, and the fretted sunlight through the swaying branches of an old plane tree. But Donald has seen his Lord hanging upon the Cross for him, and the New Jerusalem descending like a bride adorned for her husband more plainly than if Perugino's great Crucifixion, with the kneeling saints, and Angelico's Outer Court of Heaven, with the dancing angels, had been hung in our little Free Kirk. When he went down the aisle with the flagon in the Sacrament, he walked as one in a dream, and wist not that his face shone.

There was an interval after the Sacrament, when the

stranger was sent to his room with light refreshments, to prepare himself for the evening, and the elders dined with the minister. Before the introduction of the Highlanders conversation had an easy play within recognized limits, and was always opened by Burnbrae, who had come out in '43, and was understood to have read the Confession of Faith.

"Ye gave us a grawnd discoorse this mornin', sir, baith instructive and edifyin'; we were juist sayin' comin' up the gairden that ye were never heard to mair advantage."

The minister was much relieved, because he had not been hopeful during the week, and was still dissatisfied, as he explained at length, with the passage on the Colossian heresy.

When these doubts had been cleared up, Burnbrae did his best by the minister up stairs, who had submitted himself to the severe test of table addresses.

"Yon were verra suitable words at the second table; he's a speeritually minded man, Maister Cosh, and has the richt sough."

Or at the worst, when Burnbrae's courage had failed:

"Maister McKittrick had a fine text afore the table. I aye like tae see a man gang tae the Song o' Solomon on the Sacrament Sabbath. A' mind Dr. Guthrie on that verra subject twenty years syne."

Having paid its religious dues, conversation was now allowed some freedom, and it was wonderful how many things could be touched on , always from a sacramental standpoint.

"We've been awfu' favoured wi' weather the day, and ought to be thankfu'. Gin it hads on like this I wudna say but th'ill be a gude hairst. That's a fine pucklie aits ye hae in the laigh park, Burnbrae."

"A've seen waur; they're fillin' no that bad. I wes juist thinkin' as I cam to the Kirk that there wes aits in that field the Sacrament after the Disruption."

"Did ye notice that Rachel Skene sat in her seat through the tables? Says I, 'Are ye no gain forrit, Mistress Skene, or hae ye lost yir token?' 'Na, na,' says she, 'ma token's safe in ma handkerchief; but I cudna get to Kirk yesterday, and I never went forrit withoot ma Saiturday yet, and I'm no to begin noo.'"

"She was aye a richt-thinkin' woman, Rachel, there's nae mistake o' that; a' wonder hoo her son is gettin' on wi' that fairm he's takin'; a' doot it's rack-rented."

It was an honest, satisfying conversation, and reminded one of the parish of Drumtochty, being both *quoad sacra* and *quoad civilia*.

When the Highlanders came in, Burnbrae was deposed after one encounter, and the minister was reduced to a state of timid suggestion. There were days when they would not speak one word, and were understood to be lost in meditation; on others they broke in on any conversation that was going from levels beyond the imagination of Drumtochty. Had this happened in the Auld Manse, Drumsheugh would have taken for granted that Donald was "feeling sober" (ill), and recommended the bottle which cured him of "a hoast" (cough) in the fifties. But the Free Kirk had been taught that the Highlanders were unapproachable in spiritual attainments, and even Burnbrae took his discipline meekly.

"It wes a mercy the mune changed last week, Maister Menzies, or a'm thinkin' it hed been a weet sacrament."

Donald came out of a maze, where he had been wandering in great peace.

"I wass not hearing that the moon had anything to do in the matter. Oh no, but he wass bound hand and foot by a mighty man."

"Wha was bund? A'm no juist followin' ye, Maister Menzies."

"The Prince of the power of the air. Oh yes, and he shall not be loosed till the occasion be over. I hef had a sign." After which conversation on the weather languished.

Perhaps the minister fared worse in an attempt to extract a certificate of efficiency from Lachlan Campbell in favour of a rhetorical young preacher.

"A fery nice speaker, and well pleased with himself. But I would be thinking, when he wass giving his images. Oh yes, I would be thinking. There wass a laddie feeshing in the burn before my house, and a fery pretty laddie he wass. He had a rod and a string, and he threw his line peautiful. It wass a great peety he had no hook, for it iss a want, and you do not catch many fish without a hook. But I shall be glad that you are pleased, sir, and all the elders."

These were only passing incidents, and left no trace, but the rebuke Donald gave to Burnbrae will be told while an elder lives. One of the last of the old mystical school, which trace their descent from Samuel Rutherford, had described the great mystery of our Faith with such insight and pathos, that Donald had stood by the table weeping gently, and found himself afterwards in the manse, he knew not how.

The silence was more than could be borne, and his former responsibility fell on Burnbrae.

"It wes wonnerful, and I canna mind hearing the like o' yon at the tables; but I wes sorry to see the Doctor sae failed. He wes bent twa fad; a' doot it's a titch o' rheumatism, or maybe lumbago."

Johannine men are subject to sudden flashes of anger, and Donald blazed.

"Bent down with rheumatism, iss that what you say? Oh yes, it will be rheumatism. Hass the sight of your eyes left you, and hef you no discernment? Did ye not see that he was bowed to the very table with the power of the Word? for it was a fire in his bones, and he was baptised with the Holy Ghost."

When the elders gathered in the vestry, the minister asked what time the preacher might have for his evening sermon, and Donald again burst forth:

"I am told that in towns the Gospel goes by minutes, like the trains at the stations; but there iss no time-table here, for we shall wait till the sun goes down to hear all things God will be sending by His servant."

Good memories differ about the text that Sacrament evening, and the length of the sermon, but all hold as a treasure for ever what happened when the book was closed. The people were hushed into a quiet that might be felt, and the old man, swayed by the spirit of the Prophets, began to repeat the blessings and curses in the Bible between Genesis and Revelation, and after each pair he cried with heart-piercing voice, "Choose this day which ye will take," till Donald could contain himself no longer.

"Here iss the man who hass deserved all the curses, and here iss the man who chooses all the blessings."

Our fathers had no turn for sensation, but they had an unerring sense of a spiritual situation. The preacher paused for five seconds, while no man could breathe, and then lifting up his hand to Heaven he said, with an indescribable authority and tenderness, "The Lord fulfil the desire of your heart both in this world and in that which is to come."

Then the congregation sang, after the ancient custom of our parts,

> "Now blessed be the Lord our God,
> The God of Israel,"

and Donald's face was one glory, because he saw in the soft evening light of the upper window the angels of God ascending and descending upon the Son of man.

It was after this that the Free Kirk minister occupied six months in proving that Moses did not write Deuteronomy, and Lachlan was trying for the same period to have the minister removed from Drumtochty.

Ian Maclaren

Donald, deprived by one stroke of both his friends, fell back on me, and told me many things I loved to hear, although they were beyond my comprehension.

"It wass not always so with me as it iss this day, for I once had no ear for God's voice, and my eyes were holden that I saw not the spiritual world. But sore sickness came upon me, and I wass nigh unto death, and my soul awoke within me and began to cry like a child for its mother. All my days I had lived on Loch Tay, and now I thought of the other country into which I would hef to be going, where I had no nest, and my soul would be driven to and fro in the darkness as a bird on the moor of Rannoch.

"Janet sent for the minister, and he wass fery kind, and he spoke about my sickness and my farm, and I said nothing. For I wass hoping he would tell me what I wass to do for my soul. But he began upon the sheep market at Amulree, and I knew he wass also in the dark. After he left I turned my face to the wall and wept.

"Next morning wass the Sabbath, and I said to Janet:

"'Wrap me in my plaid, and put me in a cart, and take me to Aberfeldy.' 'And what will ye be doing at Aberfeldy? and you will die on the road.' 'There iss,' said I, 'a man there who knows the way of the soul, and it iss better to die with my face to the light.'

"They set me in a corner of the church where I wass thinking no man could see me, and I cried in my heart without ceasing, 'Lord, send me - send me a word from Thy mouth.'

"When the minister came into the pulpit he gave me a strange look, and this wass his text, 'Loose him and let him go.'

"As he preached I knew I wass Lazurus, with the darkness of the grave around me, and my soul straitly bound. I could do nothing, but I wass longing with all my strength.

"Then the minister stopped, and he said:

"There iss a man in this church, and he will know himself who it iss. When I came in this morning I saw a shadow on his face, and I knew not whether it was the wing of the Angel of Life or the Angel of Death passing over him, but the Lord has made it plain to me, and I see the silver feathers of the Angel of the Covenant, and this shall be a sign unto that man, 'Loose him and let him go.'"

"While he wass still speaking I felt my soul carried out into the light of God's face, and my grave clothes were taken off one by one as Janet would unwind my plaid, and I stood a living man before Christ.

"It wass a sweet June day as we drove home, and I lay in sunshine, and every bird that sang, and the burnies by the roadside, and the rustling of the birch leaves in the wind - oh yes, and the sound of the horse's feet were saying, 'Loose him and let him go.'

"Loch Tay looked black angry as we came by its side in the morning, and I said to Janet:

"'It iss the Dead Sea, and I shall be as Sodom and Gomorrah;' but in the evening it wass as a sea of glass

mingled with fire, and I heard the song of Moses and
the Lamb sweeping over the Loch, but this wass still
the sweetest word to me, 'Loose him and let him go.'"

II

AGAINST PRINCIPALITIES AND POWERS

The powers of darkness had been making a dead set upon Donald all winter, and towards spring he began to lose hope. He came to the Cottage once a week with news from the seat of war, and I could distinguish three zones of depression. Within the first he bewailed his inveterate attachment to this world, and his absolute indifference to spiritual things, and was content to describe himself as Achan. The sign that he had entered the second was a recurring reference to apostacy, and then you had the melancholy satisfaction of meeting the living representative of Simon Peter. When he passed into the last zone of the Purgatorio, Donald was beyond speech, and simply allowed one to gather from allusions to thirty pieces of silver that he was Judas Iscariot.

So long as it was only Achan or Simon Peter that came to sit with me, one was not gravely concerned, but Judas Iscariot meant that Donald had entered the Valley of the Shadow.

He made a spirited rally at the Winter Sacrament, and distinguished himself greatly on the evening of the Fast day. Being asked to pray, as a recognition of comparative cheerfulness, Donald continued for five and twenty minutes, and unfolded the works of the Devil in such minute and vivid detail that Burnbrae talks about it to this day, and Lachlan Campbell, although an expert in this department, confessed astonishment. It was a mighty wrestle, and it was perhaps natural that Donald should groan heavily at regular intervals, and acquaint the meeting how the conflict went, but the younger people were much shaken, and the edification even of the serious was not without reserve.

While Donald still lingered on the field of battle to gather the spoils and guard against any sudden return of the enemy, the elders had a hurried consultation in the vestry, and Burnbrae put the position with admirable force.

"Naebody can deny that it wes a maist extraordinary prayer, and it passes me hoo he kens sae muckle aboot the Deevil. In fac' it's a preevilege tae hae sic an experienced hand among us, and I wudna offend Donald Menzies for onything. But yon groanin' wes a wee thingie discomposin', and when he said, kind o' confidential, 'He's losing his grup,' ma ain fouk cudna keep their coontenance. Weel, I wes thinkin' that the best plan wud be for Maister Campbell juist tae give a bit advice and tell Donald that we're thankfu' to hear him at the meeting, and michty lifted wi' his peteetions, but it wud be an obleegation gin he wud leave oot the groans and tell us aifterwards what wes gaein' on, maybe in the Session."

Lachlan accepted his commission with quite unusual diffidence, and offered a very free translation on the way home.

"It wass a mercy to hef you at the meeting this night, Donald Menzies, for I saw that Satan had come in great strength, and it iss not every man that can withstand him. But you will not be ignorant of his devices; oh no, you will be knowing them fery well. Satan had not much to say before the prayer wass done, and I will not be expecting to see him again at this occasion. It wass the elders said, 'Donald Menzies hass trampled Satan under foot.' Oh yes, and fery glad men they were, for it iss not given to them. But I would be thinking iss it good to let the Devil hear you groaning in the battle, and I would be wishing that you had kept all your groans and given them to me on the road."

"Iss it the groans you are not liking?" retorted Donald, stung by this unexpected criticism. "And what iss wrong with groaning? But I hef the Scripture, and I will not be caring what you say, Lachlan Campbell."

"If you hef a warrant for groaning, it iss this man that will be glad to hear it, for I am not remembering that passage."

"Maybe you hef not read 'Maketh intercession with groanings,' but it iss a fery good Scripture, and it iss in my Bible."

"All Scripture iss good, Donald Menzies, but it iss not lawful to divide Scripture, and it will read in my Bible, 'groanings which cannot be uttered,' and I wass saying this would be the best way with your groans."

Donald came in to tell me how his companion in arms had treated him, and was still sore.

"He iss in the bondage of the letter these days, for he will be always talking about Moses with the minister, and I am not hearing that iss good for the soul."

If even Lachlan could not attain to Donald, it was perhaps no discredit that the Drumtochty mind was at times hopelessly perplexed.

"He's a gude cratur and terrible gifted in prayer," Netherton explained to Burnbrae after a prayer-meeting, when Donald had temporarily abandoned Satan and given himself to autobiography, "but yon wesna a verra ceevil way to speak aboot his faither and mither."

"A' doot yir imaginin', Netherton. Donald never mentioned his fouk the nicht, and it's no likely he wud in the prayer-meeting."

"There's nae imaginin' aboot it; a' heard him wi' ma ain ears say twice, 'My father was an Amorite, and my mother a Hittite.' I'll take my aith on it. Noo, a' dinna ken Donald's forbears masel, for he's frae Tayside, but supposin' they were as bad as bad cud be, it's no for him to blacken his ain blood, and him an Elder."

"Toots, Netherton, yir aff it a' thegither. Div ye no see yon's Bible langidge oot o' a Prophet, or maybe Kings, and Donald wes usin't in a feegurative capaucity?"

"Feegurative or no feegurative, Burnbrae, it disna maitter; it's a peetifu' job howking (digging) thro' the Bible for ill words tae misca yir fouk wi' afore the public."

Burnbrae gave up the contest in despair, feeling

himself that Old Testament allusions were risky, and that Donald's quotation was less than felicitous.

Donald's prayers were not known outside the Free Kirk circle, but his encounters with the evil one were public property, and caused a general shudder. Drumtochty was never sure who might not be listening, and considered that it was safer not to meddle with certain nameless people. But Donald waged an open warfare in every corner of the parish, in the Kirk, by the wayside, in his house, on the road to market, and was ready to give any one the benefit of his experiences.

"Donald Menzies is in yonder," said Hillocks, pointing to the smithy, whose fire sent fitful gleams across the dark road, "and he's carryin' on maist fearsome. Ye wud think tae hear him speak that auld Hornie wes gaein' louse in the parish; it sent a grue (shiver) doon ma back. Faigs, it's no cannie to be muckle wi' the body, for the Deil and Donald seem never separate. Hear him noo, hear him."

"Oh yes," said Donald, addressing the smith and two horror-stricken ploughmen, "I hef seen him, and he hass withstood me on the road. It wass late, and I wass thinking on the shepherd and the sheep, and Satan will come out from the wood below Hillocks' farm-house ('Gude preserve us,' from Hillocks) and say, 'That word is not for you, Donald Menzies,' But I wass strong that night, and I said, 'Neither shall any pluck them out of my hand,' and he will not wait long after that, oh no, and I did not follow him into the wood."

The smith, released by the conclusion of the tale, blew a mighty blast, and the fire burst into a red blaze, throwing into relief the black figure of the smith and

Ian Maclaren

the white faces of the ploughmen; glancing from the teeth of harrows, and the blades of scythes, and the cruel knives of reaping machines, and from instruments with triple prongs; and lighting up with a hideous glare the black sooty recesses of the smithy.

"Keep's a'," whispered Hillocks, clutching my arm, "it's little better than the ill place. I wish to gudeness I wes safe in ma ain hoose."

These were only indecisive skirmishes, for one evening Donald came to my den with despair written on every feature, and I knew that fighting had begun at the centre, and that he was worsted.

It was half an hour before he became articulate, during which time he sighed as if the end of all things had come, and I caught the word scapegoat twice, but at last he told me that he had resigned his eldership, and would absent himself in future from the Free Kirk.

"It hass been a weary winter when minister and people hef gone into captivity, and on Sabbath the word wass taken altogether from the minister's mouth, and he spake a language which we understood not [it was the first of three sermons on the Hexateuch, and had treated of the Jehovistic and Elohistic documents with much learning], and I will be asking all the way back, 'Iss it I?' 'Iss it I?'

"Oh yes, and when I opened my Bible this iss the word I will see, 'That thou doest do quickly,' and I knew it wass my sins that had brought great judgments on the people, and turned the minister into a man of stammering lips and another tongue.

"It wass a mercy that the roof did not fall and bury all the people with me; but we will not be tempting the Almighty, for I hef gone outside, and now there will be peace and blessing."

When we left the lighted room and stood on the doorstep, Donald pointed to the darkness. "There iss no star, and you will be remembering what John saw when the door opened and Judas went out. 'It wass night' - oh yes, it iss night for me, but it will be light for them."

As weeks went past, and Donald was seen neither at Kirk nor market, my heart went out to the lonely man in his soul conflict, and, although there was no help in me, I went to ask how it fared with him. After the footpath disentangled itself from the pine woods and crossed the burn by two fir trees nailed together, it climbed a steep ascent to Donald's house, but I had barely touched the foot, when I saw him descending, his head in the air, and his face shining. Before any words passed, I knew that the battle had been fought and won.

"It wass last night, and I will be coming to tell you. Satan hass gone like darkness when the sun ariseth, and I hef been delivered."

There are stories one cannot hear sitting, and so we paced the meadow below, rich in primroses, with a sloping bank of gorse behind us, and the pines before us, and the water breaking over the stones at our feet.

"It is three weeks since I saw you, and all that time I hef been wandering on the hill by day, and lying in the barn at night, for it wass not good to be with people,

Ian Maclaren

and Satan wass always saying to me, Judas went to 'his own place.' My dog will lay his head on my knee, and be sorry for me, and the dumb animals will be looking at me out of their great eyes, and be moaning.

"The lads are good singers, and there wass always a sound of Psalms on the farm, oh yes, and it was pleasant to come from the market and hear the Psalms at the foot of the hill. It wass like going up to Jerusalem. But there would be no Psalms these days, for the lads could not sing when their father's soul wass going down into the pit.

"Oh no, and there wass no prayer last night, but I told the lads to go to bed, and I lay down before the fire to wrestle once more before I perished.

"Janet will offer this word and the other, and I will be trying them all, but Satan wass tearing them away as quick as I could speak, and he always said, 'his own place.'

"'There iss no hope for me,' I cried, 'but it iss a mercy that you and the lads will be safe in the City, and maybe the Lord will let me see you all through the gate.' And that wass lifting me, but then I will hear 'his own place,' 'his own place,' and my heart began to fail, and I wass nigh to despair.

"Then I heard a voice, oh yes, as plain as you are hearing me, 'The blood of Jesus Christ, His Son, cleanseth us from all sin.' It wass like a gleam from the Mercy-seat, but I would be waiting to see whether Satan had any answer, and my heart was standing still. But there wass no word from him, not one word. Then I leaped to my feet and cried, 'Get thee behind me,

Satan,' and I will look round, and there wass no one to be seen but Janet in her chair, with the tears on her cheeks, and she wass saying, 'Thanks be to God, which giveth us the victory through our Lord Jesus Christ.'

"The lads were not sleeping fery sound when their father was fighting for his life, oh no, and I am not saying but maybe they would be praying. It wass not fery long before they came down, and Hamish will be looking at my face, and then he will get the books, and this is the Psalm we sang?

> "I love the Lord, because my voice
> And prayers He did hear.
> I, while I live, will call on Him,
> Who bowed to me His ear.

> *   *   *   *   *

> God merciful and righteous is,
> Yea, gracious is our Lord;
> God saves the meek; I was brought low,
> He did me help afford."

This was the victory of Donald Menzies, and on reaching home I marked that the early roses were beginning to bloom over the door through which Donald had gone out into the darkness.

HIS MOTHER'S SERMON

He was an ingenuous lad, with the callow simplicity of a theological college still untouched, and had arrived on the preceding Monday at the Free Kirk manse with four cartloads of furniture and a maiden aunt. For three days he roamed from room to room in the excitement of householding, and made suggestions which were received with hilarious contempt; then he shut himself up in his study to prepare the great sermon, and his aunt went about on tiptoe. During meals on Friday he explained casually that his own wish was to preach a simple sermon, and that he would have done so had he been a private individual, but as he had held the MacWhammel scholarship a deliverance was expected by the country. He would be careful and say nothing rash, but it was due to himself to state the present position of theological thought, and he might have to quote once or twice from Ewald.

His aunt was a saint, with that firm grasp of truth, and tender mysticism, whose combination is the charm of Scottish piety, and her face was troubled. While the minister was speaking in his boyish complacency, her thoughts were in a room where they had both stood, five years before, by the death-bed of his mother.

He was broken that day, and his sobs shook the bed, for he was his mother's only son and fatherless, and his mother, brave and faithful to the last, was bidding him farewell.

"Dinna greet like that, John, nor break yir hert, for it's the will o' God, and that's aye best."

"Here's my watch and chain," placing them beside her son, who could not touch them, nor would lift his head, "and when ye feel the chain about yir neck it will mind ye o' yir mother's arms."

"Ye 'ill no forget me, John, I ken that weel, and I'll never forget you. I've loved ye here and I'll love ye yonder. Th'ill no be an 'oor when I'll no pray for ye, and I'll ken better what to ask than I did here, sae dinna be comfortless."

Then she felt for his head and stroked it once more, but he could not look nor speak.

"Ye 'ill follow Christ, and gin He offers ye His cross, ye 'ill no refuse it, for He aye carries the heavy end Himsel'. He's guided yir mother a' thae years, and been as gude as a husband since yir father's death, and He 'ill hold me fast tae the end. He 'ill keep ye too, and, John, I'll be watchin' for ye. Ye 'ill no fail me," and her poor cold hand that had tended him all his days tightened on his head.

But he could not speak, and her voice was failing fast.

"I canna see ye noo, John, but I know yir there, and I've just one other wish. If God calls ye to the ministry, ye 'ill no refuse, an' the first day ye preach in yir ain kirk, speak a gude word for Jesus Christ, an,' John, I'll hear ye that day , though ye 'ill no see me , and I'll

Ian Maclaren

be satisfied."

A minute after she whispered, "Pray for me," and he cried, "My mother, my mother."

It was a full prayer, and left nothing unasked of Mary's Son.

"John," said his aunt, "your mother is with the Lord," and he saw death for the first time, but it was beautiful with the peace that passeth all understanding.

Five years had passed, crowded with thought and work, and his aunt wondered whether he remembered that last request, or indeed had heard it in his sorrow.

"What are you thinking about, aunt? Are you afraid of my theology?"

"No, John, it's no that, laddie, for I ken ye 'ill say what ye believe to be true withoot fear o' man," and she hesitated.

"Come, out with it, auntie: you're my only mother now, you know," and the minister put his arm round her, "as well as the kindest, bonniest, goodest auntie ever man had."

Below his student self-conceit he was a good lad, and sound of heart.

"Shame on you, John, to make a fule o' an auld dune body, but ye'll no come round me with yir flattery. I ken ye ower weel," and as she caught the likeness in his face, her eyes filled suddenly.

"What's the matter, auntie? Will ye no tell me?"

"Dinna be angry wi' me, John, but a'm concerned aboot Sabbath, for a've been praying ever syne ye were called to Drumtochty that it micht be a great day, and that I micht see ye comin' tae yir people, laddie, wi' the beauty o' the Lord upon ye, according tae the auld prophecy: 'How beautiful upon the mountains are the feet of him that bringeth good tidings, that publisheth peace,'" and again she stopped.

"Go on, auntie, go on," he whispered; "say all that's in yir mind."

"It's no for me tae advise ye, who am only a simple auld woman, who ken's naethin' but her Bible and the Catechism, and it's no that a'm feared for the new views, or aboot yir faith, for I aye mind that there's mony things the Speerit hes still tae teach us, and I ken weel the man that follows Christ will never lose his way in ony thicket. But it's the fouk, John, a'm anxious aboot, the flock o' sheep the Lord hes given ye tae feed for Him."

She could not see his face, but she felt him gently press her hand, and took courage.

"Ye maun mind, laddie, that they're no clever and learned like what ye are, but juist plain country fouk, ilka ane wi' his ain temptation, an' a' sair trachled wi' mony cares o' this world. They 'ill need a clear word tae comfort their herts and show them the way everlasting. Ye 'ill say what's richt, nae doot o' that, and a'body 'ill be pleased wi' ye, but, oh, laddie, be sure ye say a gude word for Jesus Christ."

Ian Maclaren

The minister's face whitened, and his arm relaxed. He rose hastily and went to the door, but in going out he gave his aunt an understanding look, such as passes between people who have stood together in a sorrow. The son had not forgotten his mother's request.

The manse garden lies toward the west, and as the minister paced its little square of turf, sheltered by fir hedges, the sun was going down behind the Grampians. Black massy clouds had begun to gather in the evening, and threatened to obscure the sunset, which was the finest sight a Drumtochty man was ever likely to see, and a means of grace to every sensible heart in the glen. But the sun had beat back the clouds on either side, and shot them through with glory and now between piled billows of light he went along a shining pathway into the Gates of the West. The minister stood still before that spectacle, his face bathed in the golden glory, and then before his eyes the gold deepened into an awful red, and the red passed into shades of violet and green, beyond painter's hand or the imagination of man. It seemed to him as if a victorious saint had entered through the gates into the city, washed in the blood of the Lamb, and the after glow of his mother's life fell solemnly on his soul. The last trace of sunset had faded from the hills when the minister came in, and his face was of one who had seen a vision. He asked his aunt to have worship with the servant, for he must be alone in his study.

It was a cheerful room in the daytime, with its southern window, through which the minister saw the roses touching the very glass and dwarf apple trees lining the garden walks; there was also a western window that he might watch each day close. It was a pleasant room now, when the curtains were drawn, and the light of the lamp fell on the books he loved, and which bade him welcome. One by one he had arranged the hard-bought treasures of student days in the little book-case, and had planned for himself that sweetest of pleasures, an evening of desultory reading. But his books went out of mind as he looked at the sermon shining beneath the glare of the lamp, and demanding judgment. He had finished its last page with honest pride that afternoon, and had declaimed it, facing the southern window, with a success that amazed himself. His hope was that he might be kept humble, and not called to Edinburgh for at least two years; and now he lifted the sheets with fear. The brilliant opening, with its historical parallel, this review of modern thought reinforced by telling quotations, that trenchant criticism of old-fashioned views, would not deliver. For the audience had vanished, and left one careworn, but ever beautiful face, whose gentle eyes were waiting with a yearning look. Twice he crushed the sermon in his hands, and turned to the fire his aunt's care had kindled, and twice he repented and smoothed it out. What else could he say now to the people? and then in the stillness of the room he heard a voice, "Speak a gude word for Jesus Christ."

Next minute he was kneeling on the hearth, and pressing the *magnum opus*, that was to shake Drumtochty, into the heart of the red fire, and he saw, half-smiling and half-weeping, the impressive words, "Semitic environment," shrivel up and disappear. As the last black flake fluttered out of sight, the face looked at him again, but this time the sweet brown eyes were full of peace.

It was no masterpiece, but only the crude production of a lad who knew little of letters and nothing of the world. Very likely it would have done neither harm nor good, but it was his best, and he gave it for love's sake, and I suppose that there is nothing in a human life so precious to God, neither clever words nor famous deeds, as the sacrifices of love.

The moon flooded his bedroom with silver light, and he felt the presence of his mother. His bed stood ghostly with its white curtains, and he remembered how every night his mother knelt by its side in prayer for him. He is a boy once more, and repeats the Lord's Prayer, then he cries again, "My mother! my mother!" and an indescribable contentment fills his heart.

His prayer next morning was very short, but afterwards he stood at the window for a space, and when he turned, his aunt said:

"Ye will get yir sermon, and it will be worth hearing."

"How did ye know?"

But she only smiled, "I heard you pray."

When he shut himself into the study that Saturday morning, his aunt went into her room above, and he knew she had gone to intercede for him.

An hour afterwards he was pacing the garden in such anxious thought that he crushed with his foot a rose lying on the path, and then she saw his face suddenly lighten, and he hurried to the house, but first he plucked a bunch of forget-me-nots. In the evening she found them on his sermon.

Two hours later - for still she prayed and watched in

faithfulness to mother and son - she observed him come out and wander round the garden in great joy. He lifted up the soiled rose and put it in his coat; he released a butterfly caught in some mesh; he buried his face in fragrant honeysuckle. Then she understood that his heart was full of love, and was sure that it would be well on the morrow.

When the bell began to ring, the minister rose from his knees and went to his aunt's room to be robed, for this was a covenant between them.

His gown was spread out in its black silken glory, but he sat down in despair.

"Auntie, whatever shall we do, for I've forgotten the bands?"

"But I've not forgot them, John, and here are six pair wrought with my own hands, and now sit still and I'll tie them round my laddie's neck."

When she had given the last touch, and he was ready to go, a sudden seriousness fell upon them.

"Kiss me, auntie."

"For your mother, and her God be with you," and then he went through the garden and underneath the honeysuckle and into the kirk, where every Free Churchman in Drumtochty that could get out of bed, and half the Established Kirk, were waiting in expectation.

I sat with his aunt in the minister's pew, and shall always be glad that I was at that service. When winter

Ian Maclaren

lies heavy upon the glen I go upon my travels, and in my time have seen many religious functions. I have been in Mr. Spurgeon's Tabernacle, where the people wept one minute and laughed the next; have heard Canon Liddon in St. Paul's, and the sound of that high, clear voice is still with me, "Awake, awake, put on thy strength, O Zion;" have seen High Mass in St. Peter's, and stood in the dusk of the Duomo at Florence when Padre Agostino thundered against the evils of the day. But I never realised the unseen world as I did that day in the Free Kirk of Drumtochty.

It is impossible to analyse a spiritual effect, because it is largely an atmosphere, but certain circumstances assisted. One was instantly prepossessed in favour of a young minister who gave out the second paraphrase at his first service, for it declared his filial reverence and won for him the blessing of a cloud of witnesses. No Scottish man can ever sing,

> "God of our fathers, be the God
> Of their succeeding race."

with a dry heart. It satisfied me at once that the minister was of a fine temper when, after a brave attempt to join, he hid his face and was silent. We thought none the worse of him that he was nervous, and two or three old people who had suspected self-sufficiency took him to their hearts when the minister concluded the Lord's prayer hurriedly, having omitted two petitions. But we knew it was not nervousness which made him pause for ten seconds after praying for widows and orphans, and in the silence which fell upon us the Divine Spirit had free access. His youth commended him, since he was also modest, for every mother had come with an inarticulate prayer that the "puir laddie wud dae weel on his first day, and him only twenty-four." Texts I can never remember, nor, for that matter, the words of sermons; but the subject was Jesus Christ, and before he had spoken five minutes I was convinced, who am outside dogmas and churches, that Christ was present. The preacher faded from before one's eyes, and there rose the figure of the Nazarene, best lover of every human soul, with a face of tender patience such as Sarto gave the Master in the Church of the Annunziata, and stretching out His hands to old folk and little children as He did, before His death, in Galilee. His voice might be heard any moment, as I have imagined it in my lonely hours by the winter fire or on the solitary hills - soft, low, and sweet, penetrating like music to the secret of the heart, "Come unto Me ... and I will give you rest."

During a pause in the sermon I glanced up the church, and saw the same spell held the people. Donald Menzies had long ago been caught into the third heaven, and was now hearing words which it is not lawful to utter. Campbell in his watch-tower at the back had closed his eyes, and was praying. The women were weeping quietly, and the rugged faces of our men were subdued and softened, as when the evening sun plays on the granite stone.

But what will stand out for ever before my mind was the sight of Marget Howe. Her face was as white as death, and her wonderful grey eyes were shining through a mist of tears, so that I caught the light in the manse pew. She was thinking of George, and had taken the minister to her heart.

The elders, one by one, gripped the minister's hand in the vestry, and, though plain, homely men, they were the godliest in the glen; but no man spoke save Burnbrae.

"I a' but lost ae fairm for the Free Kirk, and I wud hae lost ten tae be in the Kirk this day."

Donald walked with me homewards, but would only say:

"There was a man sent from God whose name was John." At the cottage he added, "The friend of the bridegroom rejoiced greatly because of the bridegroom's voice,"

Beneath the honeysuckle at his garden gate a woman was waiting.

"My name is Marget Howe, and I'm the wife of William Howe of Whinnie Knowe. My only son wes preparin' for the ministry, but God wanted him nearly a year syne. When ye preached the Evangel o' Jesus the day I heard his voice, and I loved you. Ye hev nae mither on earth, I hear, and I hae nae son, and I wantit tae say that if ye ever wish tae speak to ony woman as ye wud tae yir mither, come tae Whinnie Knowe, an' I'll coont it ane of the Lord's consolations."

His aunt could only meet him in the study, and when he looked on her his lip quivered, for his heart was wrung with one wistful regret.

"Oh, auntie, if she had only been spared to see this day, and her prayers answered."

But his aunt flung her arms round his neck.

"Dinna be cast doon, laddie, nor be unbelievin'. Yir mither has heard every word, and is satisfied, for ye did it in remembrance o' her, and yon was yir mither's sermon."

THE TRANSFORMATION OF
LACHLAN CAMPBELL

I

A GRAND INQUISITOR

The Free Kirk of Drumtochty had no gallery, but a section of seats at the back was raised two feet, and any one in the first pew might be said to sit in the "briest o' the laft." When Lachlan Campbell arrived from the privileged parish of Auchindarroch, where the "Men" ruled with iron hand and no one shaved on Sabbath, he examined the lie of country with the eye of a strategist, and seized at once a corner seat on the crest of the hill. From this vantage ground, with his back to the wall and a clear space left between himself and his daughter Flora, he had an easy command of the pulpit, and within six months had been constituted a court of review neither minister nor people could lightly disregard. It was not that Lachlan spoke hastily or at length, for his policy was generally a silence pregnant with judgment, and his deliverances were for the most part in parables, none the less awful because hard of interpretation. Like every true Celt, he had the power of reserve, and knew the value of mystery. His voice must not be heard in irresponsible gossip at the Kirk door, and he never condescended to the level of Mrs. MacFadyen, our recognised sermon taster, who criticised everything in the technique of the pulpit, from the number of heads in a sermon to the air with which a probationer used his pocket-handkerchief. She lived in the eye of the public, and gave her opinions with the light heart of a newspaper writer; but Lachlan kept himself in the shadow and wore a manner of studied humility as became the administrator of the Holy Office in Drumtochty.

Lachlan was a little man, with a spare, wiry body, iron grey hair and whiskers carefully arranged, a keen, old-fashioned face sharpened by much spiritual thinking, and eyes that looked at you from beneath shaggy eyebrows as from some other world. His face had an irresistible suggestion of a Skye terrier, the most serious of animals, with the hair reduced, and Drumsheugh carried us all with him when, in a moment of inspiration, he declared that "the body looks as if he hed juist come oot o' the Ark." He was a shepherd to trade, and very faithful in all his work, but his life business was theology, from Supralapsarianism in Election to the marks of faith in a believer's heart. His library consisted of some fifty volumes of ancient divinity, and lay on an old oak kist close to his hand, where he sat beside the fire of a winter night. When the sheep were safe and his day's labour was over, he read by the light of the fire and the "crusie" (oil-lamp) overhead, Witsius on the Covenants, or Rutherford's "Christ Dying," or Bunyan's "Grace Abounding," or Owen's "130th Psalm," while the collies slept at his feet, and Flora put the finishing stroke to some bit of rustic finery. Worship was always coloured by the evening's reading, but the old man never forgot to pray that they both might have a place in the everlasting covenant, and that the backslidings of Scotland might be healed.

As our inquisitor, Lachlan searched anxiously for sound doctrine and deep experience, but he was not concerned about learning, and fluency he regarded with disgust. When a young minister from Muirtown stamped twice in his prayer at the Drumtochty Fast, and preached with great eloquence from the words, "And there was no more sea," repeating the text at the end of each paragraph, and concluding the sermon with "Lord Ullin's Daughter," the atmosphere round Lachlan became electric, and no one dared to speak to him outside. He never expressed his mind on this melancholy exhibition, but the following Sabbath he explained the principle on which they elected ministers at Auchindarroch, which was his standard of perfection.

"Six young men came, and they did not sing songs in the pulpit. Oh no, they preached fery well, and I said to Angus Bain, 'They are all goot lads, and there is nothing wrong with their doctrine.'

"Angus wass one of the 'Men,' and saw what wass hidden from me, and he will be saying, 'Oh yes, they said their lesson fery pretty, but I did not see them tremble, Lachlan Campbell. Another iss coming, and seven is a goot number.'

"It wass next Sabbath that he came, and he wass a white man, giving out his text, 'Blessed are they which are called unto the marriage supper of the Lamb,' and I wass thinking that the Lord had laid too great a burden on the lad, and that he could not be fit for such a work. It wass not more than ten minutes before he will be trying to tell us what he wass seeing, and will not hef the words. He had to go down from the pulpit as a man that had been in the heavenly places and wass stricken dumb.

"'It iss the Lord that has put me to shame this day,' he said to the elders, 'and I will nefer show my face again in Auchindarroch, for I ought not to have meddled with things too high for me.'

"'You will show your face here every Sabbath,' answered Angus Bain, 'for the Lord said unto me, "Wait for the man that trembles at the Word, and iss not able to speak, and it will be a sign unto you,"' and a fery goot minister he wass, and made the hypocrites in Zion to be afraid."

Lachlan dealt tenderly with our young Free Kirk minister, for the sake of his first day, and passed over some very shallow experience without remark, but an autumn sermon roused him to a sense of duty. For some days a storm of wind and rain had been stripping the leaves from the trees and gathering them in sodden heaps upon the ground. The minister looked out on the garden where many holy thoughts had visited him, and his heart sank like lead, for it was desolate, and of all its beauty there remained but one rose clinging to its stalk, drenched and faded. It seemed as if youth, with its flower of promise and hope, had been beaten down, and a sense of loneliness fell on his soul. He had no heart for work, and crept to bed broken and dispirited. During the night the rain ceased, and the north wind began to blow, which cleanses nature in every pore, and braces each true man for his battle. The morrow was one of those glorious days which herald winter, and as the minister tramped along the road, where the dry leaves crackled beneath his feet, and climbed to the moor with head on high, the despair of yesterday vanished. The wind had ceased, and the glen lay at his feet, distinct in the cold, clear air, from the dark mass of pines that closed its upper end to the swelling woods of oak and beech that cut it off from the great Strath. He had received a warm welcome from all kinds of people, and now he marked with human sympathy each little homestead with its belt of firs against the winter's storms, and its stackyard where the corn had been gathered safe; the ploughman and his horses cutting brown ribbons in the bare stubble; dark squares where the potato stalks have withered to the ground, and women are raising the roots, and here and there a few cattle still out in the fields. His eye fell on the great wood through which he had rambled in August, now one blaze of colour, rich green and light yellow, with patches of fiery red and dark purple. God seemed to have given him a sermon, and he wrote that evening, like one inspired, on the same parable of nature Jesus loved, with its subtle interpretation of our sorrows, joys, trust, and hope. People told me that it was a "rael bonnie sermon," and that Netherton had forgotten his after-sermon snuff, although it was his turn to pass the box to Burnbrae.

The minister returned to his study in a fine glow of body and soul, to find a severe figure standing motionless in the middle of the room.

"Wass that what you call a sermon?" said Lachlan Campbell, without other greeting.

John Carmichael was still so full of joy that he did not catch the tone, and explained with college pedantry that it was hardly a sermon, nor yet a lecture.

"You may call it a meditation."

"I will be calling it an essay without one bite of grass for starving sheep."

Then the minister awoke from a pleasant dream, as if one had flung cold water on his naked body.

"What was wrong?" with an anxious look at the stern little man who of a sudden had become his judge.

"There wass nothing right, for I am not thinking that trees and leaves and stubble fields will save our souls, and I did not hear about sin and repentance and the work of Christ. It iss sound doctrine that we need, and a great peety you are not giving it."

The minister had been made much of in college circles, and had a fair idea of himself. He was a kindly lad, but he did not see why he should be lectured by an old Highlandman who read nothing except Puritans, and was blind with prejudice. When they parted that Sabbath afternoon it was the younger man that had lost his temper, and the other did not offer to shake hands.

Perhaps the minister would have understood Lachlan better if he had known that the old man could not touch food when he got home, and spent the evening in a fir wood praying for the lad he had begun to love. And Lachlan would have had a lighter heart if he had heard the minister questioning himself whether he had denied the Evangel or sinned against one of Christ's disciples. They argued together; they prayed apart.

Lachlan was careful to say nothing, but the congregation felt that his hand was against the minister, and Burnbrae took him to task.

"Ye maunna be ower hard on him, Maister Campbell, for he's but young, and comin' on fine. He hes a hearty word for ilka body on the road, and the sicht o' his fresh young face in the poopit is a sermon itsel'."

"You are wrong, Burnbrae, if you will be thinking that my heart iss not warm to the minister, for it went out unto him from the day he preached his first sermon. But the Lord regardeth not the countenance of man."

"Nae doot, nae doot, but I canna see onything wrang in his doctrine; it wudna be reasonable tae expect auld-fashioned sermons frae a young man, and I wud coont them barely honest. A'm no denying that he gaes far afield, and taks us tae strange lands when he's on his travels, but ye 'ill acknowledge that he gaithers mony treasures, and he aye comes back tae Christ."

"No, I will not be saying that John Carmichael does not love Christ, for I hef seen the Lord in his sermons like a face through a lattice. Oh yes, and I hef felt the fragrance of the myrrh. But I am not liking his doctrine, and I wass thinking that some day there will be no original sin left in the parish of Drumtochty."

It was about this time that the minister made a great mistake, although he was trying to do his best for the people, and always obeyed his conscience. He used to come over to the Cottage for a ramble through my books, and one evening he told me that he had prepared what he called a "course" on Biblical criticism, and was going to place Drumtochty on a level with Germany. It was certainly a strange part for me to advise a minister, but I had grown to like the lad, because he was full of enthusiasm and too honest for this world, and I implored him to be cautious.

Drumtochty was not anxious to be enlightened about the authors of the Pentateuch, being quite satisfied with Moses, and it was possible that certain good men in Drumtochty might resent any interference with their herditary notions. Why could he not read this subject for his own pleasure, and teach it quietly in classes? Why give himself away in the pulpit? This worldly counsel brought the minister to a white heat, and he rose to his feet. Had he not been ordained to feed his people with truth, and was he not bound to tell them all he knew? We were living in an age of transition, and he must prepare Christ's folk that they be not taken unawares. If he failed in his duty through any fear of consequences, men would arise afterwards to condemn him for cowardice, and lay their unbelief at his door. When he ceased I was ashamed of my cynical advice, and resolved never again to interfere with "courses" or other matters above the lay mind. But greater knowledge of the world had made me a wise prophet.

Within a month the Free Kirk was in an uproar, and when I dropped in one Sabbath morning the situation seemed to me a very pathetic tragedy. The minister was offering to the honest country folk a mass of immature and undigested details about the Bible, and they were listening with wearied, perplexed faces. Lachlan Campbell sat grim and watchful, without a sign of flinching, but even from the Manse pew I could detect the suffering of his heart. When the minister blazed into polemic against the bigotry of the old school, the iron face quivered as if a father had been struck by his son. Carmichael looked thin and nervous in the pulpit, and it came to me that if new views are to be preached to old-fashioned people it ought not to be by lads who are always heady and intolerant, but by a stout man of middle age, with a rich voice and a good-natured manner. Had Carmichael rasped and girded much longer, one would have believed in the inspiration of the vowel points, and I left the church with a low heart, for this was a woeful change from his first sermon.

Lachlan would not be pacified, not even by the plea of the minister's health.

"Oh yes, I am seeing that he is ill, and I will be as sorry as any man in Drumtochty. But it iss not too much work, as they are saying; it iss the judgment of God. It iss not goot to meddle with Moses, and John Carmichael will be knowing that. His own sister wass not respectful to Moses, and she will not be feeling fery well next day."

But Burnbrae added that the "auld man cudna be mair cast doon if he hed lost his dochter."

The peace of the Free Kirk had been broken, and the minister was eating out his heart, when he remembered the invitation of Marget Howe, and went one sweet spring day to Whinnie Knowe.

Marget met him with her quiet welcome at the garden gate.

"Ye hae dune me a great kindness in comin', Maister Carmichael, and if ye please we 'ill sit in this sunny corner which is dear tae me, and ye 'ill tell me yir troubles."

So they sat down together beside the brier bush, and after one glance at Marget's face the minister opened his heart, and told her the great controversy with Lachlan.

Marget lifted her head as one who had heard of some brave deed, and there was a ring in her voice.

"It maks me prood before God that there are twa men in Drumtochty who follow their conscience as king, and coont truth dearer than their ain freends. It's peetifu' when God's bairns fecht through greed and envy, but it's hertsome when they are wullin' tae wrestle aboot the Evangel, for surely the end o' it a' maun be peace.

"A've often thocht that in the auld days baith the man on the rack and the inqueesitor himself micht be gude men and accepted o' God, and maybe the inqueesitor suffered mair than the martyr. A'm thinkin', Maister Carmichael, that it's been hardest on Lachlan."

The minister's head was buried in his hands, but his heart was with Marget.

"It's a strange buik the Bible, and no the buik we wud hae made, tae judge by oor bit creeds and confessions. It's like a head o' aits in the harvest time. There's the ear that hauds the grain and keeps it safe, and that's the history, and there's often no mickle nutriment in it; then there's the corn lying in the ear, which is the Evangel frae Eden tae Revelation, and that is the bread o' the soul. But the corn maun be threshed first and the cauf (chaff) cleaned aff. It's a bonnie sicht tae see the pure grain fallin' like a rinnin' burn on the corn-room floor, and a glint o' the sun through the window turning it intae gold. But the stour (dust) o' the cauf room is mair than onybody can abide, and the cauf's worth naethin' when the corn's awa."

"Ye mean," said the minister, "that my study is the threshin' mill, and that some of the chaff has got into the pulpit."

"Yir no offended," and Marget's voice trembled.

Then the minister lifted his head and laughed aloud with joy, while a swift flash of humour lit up Marget's face.

"You've been the voice of God to me this day, Mrs. Howe, but if I give up my 'course,' the people will misunderstand, for I know everything I gave was true, and I would give it all again if it were expedient."

"Nae fear, Maister Carmichael, naebody misunderstands that luves, and the fouk all luve ye, and the man that hauds ye dearest is Lachlan Campbell. I saw the look in his een that canna be mista'en."

"I'll go to him this very day," and the minister leaped to his feet.

"Ye 'ill no regret it," said Marget, "for God will give ye peace."

Lachlan did not see the minister coming, for he was busy with a lamb that had lost its way and hurt itself. Carmichael marked with a growing tenderness at his heart how gently the old man washed and bound up the wounded leg, all the time crooning to the frightened creature in the sweet Gaelic speech, and also how he must needs give the lamb a drink of warm milk before he set it free.

When he rose from his work of mercy , he faced

the minister.

For an instant Lachlan hesitated, and then at the look on Carmichael's face he held out both his hands.

"This iss a goot day for me, and I bid you ten thousand welcomes."

But the minister took the first word.

"You and I, Lachlan, have not seen eye to eye about some things lately, and I am not here to argue which is nearer the truth, because perhaps we may always differ on some lesser matters. But once I spoke rudely to you, and often I have spoken unwisely in my sermons. You are an old man and I am a young, and I ask you to forgive me and to pray that both of us may be kept near the heart of our Lord, whom we love, and who loves us."

No man can be so courteous as a Celt, and Lachlan was of the pure Highland breed, kindest of friends, fiercest of foes.

"You hef done a beautiful deed this day, Maister Carmichael; and the grace of God must hef been exceeding abundant in your heart. It iss this man that asks your forgiveness, for I wass full of pride, and did not speak to you as an old man should; but God iss my witness that I would hef plucked out my right eye for your sake. You will say every word God gives you, and I will take as much as God gives me, and there will be a covenant between us as long as we live."

They knelt together on the earthen floor of that Highland cottage, the old school and the new, before

Ian Maclaren

one Lord, and the only difference in their prayers was that the young man prayed they might keep the faith once delivered unto the saints, while the burden of the old man's prayer was that they might be led into all truth.

Lachlan's portion that evening ought to have been the slaying of Sisera from the Book of Judges, but instead he read, to Flora's amazement - it was the night before she left her home - the thirteenth chapter of I Corinthians, and twice he repeated to himself, "Now we see through a glass darkly, but then face to face."

II

HIS BITTER SHAME

The Free Kirk people were very proud of their vestry because the Established Church had none, and because it was reasonably supposed to be the smallest in Scotland. When the minister, who touched five feet eleven, and the beadle, who was three inches taller, assembled for the procession, with the precentor, a man of fair proportions, there was no waste ground in that room, and any messenger from the church door had to be selected with judgment. "Step up, Airchie man, tae the vestry," Burnbrae would say to the one under-sized man in Drumtochty, "and tell the minister no tae forget the Jews. Ye can birse (push) in fine, but it wud beat me to get by the door. It's a bonnie bit room, but three fouk stannin' maks it contrakit for another man,"

It was eight feet by eight, and consisted largely of two doors and a fireplace, and its chief glory was a portrait of Dr. Chalmers, whose face, dimly seen in the light of the lamp, was a charter of authority, and raised the proceedings to the level of history. Lockers on either side of the mantelpiece contained the church library, which abounded in the lives of Scottish worthies, and was never lightly disturbed. Where there was neither grate nor door, a narrow board ran along the wall, on

Ian Maclaren

which it was simply a point of honour to seat the twelve deacons, who met once a month to raise the Sustentation Fund by modest, heroic sacrifices of hard-working people, and to keep the slates on the church roof in winter. When they had nothing else to do, they talked about the stove which "came out in '43," and, when it was in good humour, would raise the temperature in winter one degree above freezing. Seating the court was a work of art, and could only be achieved by the repression of the smaller men, who looked out from the loopholes of retreat, the projection of bigger men on to their neighbours' knees, and the absolute elimination of Archie Moncur, whose voice made motions on temperance from the lowest depths. Netherton was always the twelfth man to arrive, and nothing could be done till he was safely settled. Only some six inches were reserved at the end of the bench, and he was a full sitter, but he had discovered a trick of sitting sideways and screwing his leg against the opposite wall, that secured the court as well as himself in their places on the principle of a compressed spring. When this operation was completed, Burnbrae used to say to the minister, who sat in the middle on a cane chair before the tiniest of tables - the living was small, and the ministers never grew fat till they left -

"We're fine and comfortable noo, Moderator, and ye can begin business as sune as ye like."

As there were only six elders they could sit in state, besides leaving a vacant space for any penitents who came to confess their sins and receive absolution, or some catechumen who wished to be admitted to the sacrament. Carmichael used to say that a meeting of Session affected his imagination, and would have made an interior for Rembrandt. On one side of the table sat the men who represented the piety of the district, and were supposed to be "far ben" in the Divine fellowship, and on the other some young girl in her loneliness, who wrung her handkerchief in terror of this dreaded spiritual court, and hoped within her heart that no elder would ask her "effectual calling" from the Shorter Catechism; while the little lamp, hanging from the ceiling, and swinging gently in the wind that had free access from every airt, cast a fitful light on the fresh, tearful face of the girl and the hard, weather-beaten countenances of the elders, composed into a serious gravity not untouched by tenderness. They were little else than labouring men, but no one was elected to that court unless he had given pledges of godliness, and they bore themselves as men who had the charge of souls.

The little Sanhedrim had within it the school of Hillel, which was swayed by mercy, and its Rabbi was Burnbrae; and the school of Shammai, whose rule was inflexible justice, and its Rabbi was Lachlan Campbell. Burnbrae was a big-hearted man, with a fatherly manner, and had a genius for dealing with "young communicants."

"Weel, Jessie, we're awfu pleased tae think yer gaein' forrit, and the Dominie wes tellin' me juist last week that ye did yir work at schule graund, and knew yir Bible frae end tae end.

"It'll no be easy to speir (ask) the like o' you questions, but ye mind Abraham, Jessie."

"Ou ay," and Jessie is all alert, although she is afraid to look up.

"What was the name o' his wife, noo?"

"Sarah, an' their son was Isaac."

"That's richt, and what aboot Isaac's wife?"

"Isaac mairrit Rebecca, and they hed twa sons, Jacob and Esau," and the girl takes a shy glance at the honest elder, and begins to feel at home.

"Domsie wesna far wrang, a' see, but it's no possible ye cud tell us the names o' Jacob's sons; it's maybe no fair tae ask sic a teuch question," knowing all the while that this was a test case of Domsie's.

When Jessie reached Benjamin, Burnbrae could not contain himself.

"It's nae use trying to stick Jessie wi' the Bible, neeburs; we 'ill see what she can dae wi' the Carritches (Catechism). Yir no the lassie that said the questions frae beginning tae end wi' twa mistaks, are ye?"

Yes, she was, and dared him to come on, for Jessie has forgotten the minister and all the Session.

"The elders wud like tae hear 'What is the Lord's Supper?'"

"That's it; and, Jessie, ma woman, gie's the 'worthy receiving.'"

Jessie achieves another triumph, and is now ready for anything.

"Ye hae the Word weel stored in yir mind, lassie, and

ye maun keep it in yir life, and dinna forget that Christ's a gude Maister."

"A'll dae ma best," and Jessie declared that Burnbrae had been as kind as if she had been "his ain bairn," and that she "wasna feared ava." But her trial is not over; the worst is to come.

Lachlan began where Burnbrae ended, and very soon had Jessie on the rack.

"How old will you be?"

"Auchteen next Martinmas."

"And why will you be coming to the sacrament?"

"Ma mither thocht it was time," with a threatening of tears as she looked at the face in the corner.

"Ye will maybe tell the Session what hass been your 'lawwork' and how long ye hef been at Sinai."

"A' dinna ken what yir askin'. I was never oot o' Drumtochty," and Jessie breaks down utterly.

"A' dinna think, Moderator, we ocht tae ask sic questions," broke in Burnbrae, who could not see a little one put to confusion; "an' I canna mind them in the Gospels. There's ae commandment Jessie keeps weel, as a' can testeefy, and that's the fifth, for there's no a better dochter in Drumtochty. A' move, Moderator, she get her token; dinna greet, puir woman, for ye've dune weel, and the Session's rael satisfeed."

"It wass Dr. John's mark I wass trying the girl by,"

explained Lachlan after Jessie had gone away comforted. "And it iss a goot mark, oh yes, and very searching.

"Ye will maybe not know what it iss, Moderator," and Lachlan regarded the minister with austere superiority, for it was the winter of the feud.

No, he did not, nor any of the Session, being all douce Scotchmen, except Donald Menzies who was at home fighting the devil.

"It iss broken bones, and Dr. John did preach three hours upon it at Auchindarroch Fast, and there wass not many went to the Sacrament on that occasion.

"Broken bones iss a fine mark to begin with, and the next will be doubts. But there iss a deeper," continued Lachlan, warming to his subject, "oh yes, far deeper, and I heard of it when I wass North for the sheep, and I will not be forgetting that day with Janet Macfarlane.

"I knew she wass a professor, and I wass looking for her marks. But it wass not for me to hef been searching her; it wass that woman that should hef been trying me."

A profound silence wrapt the Session.

"'Janet,' I said, 'hef ye had many doubts?'

"'Doubts, Lachlan? was that what you asked? I hef had desertions, and one will be for six months.'

"So I saw she wass far beyond me, for I dare not be speaking about desertions."

Two minutes after the minister pronounced the benediction, and no one had offered any remark in the interval.

It seemed to the elders that Lachlan dealt hardly with young people and those that had gone astray, but they learned one evening that his justice had at least no partiality. Burnbrae said afterwards that Lachlan "looked like a ghaist comin' in at the door," but he sat in silence in the shadow, and no one marked the agony on his face till the end.

"If that iss all the business, Moderator, I hef to bring a case of discipline before the Session, and ask them to do their duty. It iss known to me that a young woman who hass been a member of this church hass left her home and gone into the far country. There will be no use in summoning her to appear before the Session, for she will never be seen again in this parish. I move that she be cut off from the roll, and her name iss " - and Lachlan's voice broke, but in an instant he recovered himself - "her name iss Flora Campbell."

Carmichael confessed to me that he was stricken dumb, and that Lachlan's ashen face held him with an awful fascination.

It was Burnbrae that first found a voice, and showed that night the fine delicacy of heart that may be hidden behind a plain exterior.

"Moderator, this is a terrible calamity that hes befaen oor brither, and a'm feelin' as if a' hed lost a bairn o' my ane, for a sweeter lassie didna cross oor kirk door. Nane o' us want tae know what hes happened or where she hes gane, and no a word o' this wull cross oor lips.

Ian Maclaren

Her faither's dune mair than cud be expeckit o' mortal man, and noo we have oor duty. It's no the way o' this Session tae cut aff ony member o' the flock at a stroke, and we 'ill no begin with Flora Campbell. A' move, Moderator, that her case be left tae her faither and yersel, and oor neebur may depend on it that Flora's name and his ain will be mentioned in oor prayers, ilka mornin' an' nicht till the gude Shepherd o' the sheep brings her hame."

Burnbrae paused, and then, with tears in his voice - men do not weep in Drumtochty - "With the Lord there is mercy, and with Him is plenteous redemption."

The minister took the old man's arm and led him into the manse, and set him in the big chair by the study fire. "Thank God, Lachlan, we are friends now; tell me about it as if I were your son and Flora's brother."

The father took a letter out of an inner pocket with a trembling hand, and this is what Carmichael read by the light of the lamp: -

"DEAR FATHER, - When this reaches you I will be in London, and not worthy to cross your door. Do not be always angry with me, and try to forgive me, for you will not be troubled any more by my dancing or dressing. Do not think that I will be blaming you, for you have been a good father to me, and said what you would be considering right, but it is not easy for a man to understand a girl. Oh, if I had had my mother, then she would have understood me, and I would not have crossed you. Forget poor Flora's foolishness, but you will not forget her, and maybe you will still pray for me. Take care of the geraniums for my sake, and give milk to the lamb that you called after me. I will never see you again, in this world or the next nor my mother ... (here the letter was much blotted). When I think that there will be no one to look after you, and have the fire burning for you on winter nights, I will be rising to come back. But it is too late, too late. Oh, the disgrace I will be bringing on you in the glen. - Your unworthy daughter,

FLORA CAMPBELL."

"This is a fiery trial, Lachlan, and I cannot even imagine what you are suffering. But do not despair, for that is not the letter of a bad girl. Perhaps she was impatient, and has been led astray. But Flora is good at heart, and you must not think she is gone forever."

Lachlan groaned, the first moan he had made, and then he tottered to his feet.

"You are fery kind, Maister Carmichael, and so wass Burnbrae, and I will be thankful you all, but you do not understand. Oh no, you do not understand." Lachlan caught hold of a chair and looked the minister in the face.

"She hass gone, and there will be no coming back. You would not take her name from the roll of the church, and I will not be meddling with that book. But I hef blotted out her name from my Bible, where her mother's name iss written and mine. She has wrought confusion in Israel and in an elder's house, and I ... I hef no danghter. But I loved her; she nefer knew how I loved her, for her mother would be looking at me from her eyes."

The minister walked with Lachlan to the foot of the

hill on which his cottage stood, and after they had shaken hands in silence, he watched the old man's figure in the cold moonlight till he disappeared into the forsaken home, where the fire had gone out on the hearth, and neither love nor hope were waiting for a broken heart.

The railway did not think it worth while to come to Drumtochty, and we, were cut off from the lowlands by miles of forest, so our manners retained the fashion of the former age. Six elders, besides the minister, knew the tragedy of Flora Campbell, and never opened their lips. Mrs. Macfadyen, who was our newspaper, and understood her duty, refused to pry into this secret. The pity of the glen went out to Lachlan, but no one even looked a question as he sat alone in his pew or came down on a Saturday afternoon to the village shop for his week's provisions. London friends thought me foolish about my adopted home, but I asked them whether they could find such perfect good manners in Belgravia, and they were silent. My Drumtochty neighbours would have played an awkward part in a drawing-room, but never have I seen in all my wanderings men and women of truer courtesy or tenderer heart.

"It gars ma hert greet tae see him," Mrs. Macfadyen said to me one day, "sae booed an' disjackit, him that wes that snod (tidy) and firm. His hair's turned white in a month, and he's awa' tae naething in his claithes. But least said is sunest mended. It's no richt tae interfere wi' another's sorrow, an' it wad be an awfu' sin tae misca' a young lassie. We maun juist houp that Flora 'll sune come back, for if she disna Lachlan 'ill no be lang wi's. He's sayin' naethin', and a' respeck him for't; but onybody can see that his hert is breakin'."

We were helpless till Marget Howe met Lachlan in the shop and read his sorrow at a glance. She went home to Whinnie Knowe in great distress.

"It wes waesome tae see the auld man githerin' his bit things wi' a shakin' hand, and speakin' tae me aboot the weather, and a' the time his eyes were sayin', 'Flora, Flora.'"

"Whar div ye think the young hizzie is, Marget?"

"Naebody needs tae know, Weelum, an' ye maunna speak that way, for whatever's come ower her, she's dear to Lachlan and tae God.

"It's laid on me tae veesit Lachlan, for a'm thinking oor Father didna comfort us withoot expeckin' that we wud comfort other fouk."

When Marget came round the corner of Lachlan's cottage, she found Flora's plants laid out in the sun, and her father watering them on his knees. One was ready to die, and for it he had made a shelter with his plaid.

He was taken unawares, but in a minute he was leading Marget in with hospitable words.

"It iss kind of you to come to an old man's house, Mistress Howe, and it iss a fery warm day. You will not care for speerits, but I am fery goot at making tea."

Marget was not as other women, and she spoke at once.

"Maister Campbell, ye will believe that I hev come in

the love of God, and because we hev baith been afflickit. I had ae son, and he is gone; ye had a dochter, and she is gone. A' ken where George is, and am sateesfied. A' doot sairly yir sorrow is deeper than mine."

"Would to God that she wass lying in the kirkyard; but I will not speak of her. She iss not anything to me this day. See, I will show you what I hef done, for she hass been a black shame to her name."

He opened the Bible, and there was Flora's name scored with wavering strokes, but the ink had run as if it had been mingled with tears.

Marget's heart burned within her at the sight, and perhaps she could hardly make allowance for Lachlan's blood and theology.

"This is what ye hev dune, and ye let a woman see yir wark. Ye are an auld man, and in sore travail, but a' tell ye before God ye hae the greater shame. Juist twenty years o' age this spring, and her mither dead. Nae woman to watch over her, and she wandered frae the fold, and a' ye can dae is to tak her oot o' yir Bible. Waes me if oor Father had blotted out oor names frae the Book o' Life when we left His hoose. But He sent His ain Son to seek us, an' a weary road He cam. A' tell ye, a man wudna leave a sheep tae perish as ye hae cast aff yir ain bairn. Yir worse than Simon the Pharisee, for Mary was nae kin tae him. Puir Flora, tae hae sic a father."

"Who will be telling you that I wass a Pharisee?" cried Lachlan, quivering in every limb, and grasping Marget's arm.

"Forgie me, Lachlan, forgie me. It was the thocht o' the misguided lassie carried me, for a' didna come tae upbraid ye."

But Lachlan had sunk into a chair and had forgotten her.

"She hass the word, and God will hef smitten the pride of my heart, for it iss Simon that I am. I wass hard on my child, and I wass hard on the minister, and there wass none like me. The Lord has laid my name in the dust, and I will be angry with her. But she iss the scapegoat for my sins, and hass gone into the desert. God be merciful to me a sinner." And then Marget understood no more, for the rest was in Gaelic, but she heard Flora's name with another she took to be her mother's twined together.

So Marget knew it would be well with Lachlan yet, and she wrote this letter:

"MY DEAR LASSIE, - Ye ken that I wes aye yir freend, and I am writing this tae say that yir father luves ye mair than ever, and is wearing oot his hert for the sicht o' yir face. Come back, or he'll dee thro' want o' his bairn. The glen is bright and bonny noo, for the purple heather is on the hills, and doon below the gowden corn, wi' bluebell and poppy flowers between. Naebody 'ill ask ye where ye've been, or onything else; there's no a bairn in the place that's no wearying tae see ye; and, Flora, lassie, if there will be sic gledness in oor wee glen when ye come hame, what think ye o' the joy in the Father's Hoose? Start the verra meenute that ye get this letter; yir father bids ye come, and I'm writing this in place o' yir mother.

MARGET HOWE."

Marget went out to tend the flowers while Lachlan read the letter, and when he gave it back the address was written in his own hand.

He went as far as the crest of the hill with Marget, and watched her on the way to the post office till she was only a speck upon the road.

When he entered his cottage the shadows were beginning to fall, and he remembered it would soon be night.

"It iss in the dark that Flora will be coming, and she must know that her father iss waiting for her."

He cleaned and trimmed with anxious hand a lamp that was kept for show, and had never been used. Then he selected from his books Edwards' "Sinners in the Hands of an angry God," and "Coles on the Divine Sovereignty," and on them he laid the large family Bible out of which Flora's name had been blotted. This was the stand on which he set the lamp in the window, and every night till Flora returned its light shone down the steep path that ascended to her home, like the Divine Love from the open door of our Father's House.

III

LIKE AS A FATHER

It was only by physical force and a free use of personalities that the Kildrummie passengers could be entrained at the Junction, and the Drumtochty men were always the last to capitulate.

They watched the main line train that had brought them from Muirtown disappear in the distance, and then broke into groups to discuss the cattle sale at leisure, while Peter, the factotum of the little Kildrummie branch, drove his way through their midst with offensive pieces of luggage, and abused them by name without respect of persons.

"It's maist aggravatin', Drumsheugh, 'at ye 'ill stand there girnin' at the prices, as if ye were a puir cottar body that hed selt her ae coo, and us twal meenutes late. Man, get intae yer kerridge; he 'ill no be fat that buys frae you, a'll wager."

"Peter's in an awfu' feery-farry (excitement) the nicht, neeburs," Drumsheugh would respond, after a long pause; "ye wud think he wes a mail gaird tae hear him speak. Mind ye, a'm no gain' tae shove ahint if the engine sticks, for I hae na time. He needs a bit nip," and Drumsheugh settles himself in his seat, "or else there wud be nae leevin' wi' him."

Peter escaped this winged shaft, for he had detected a woman in the remote darkness.

"Keep's a', wumman, what are ye stravagin' about there for out o' a body's sicht? a' near set aff withoot ye."

Then Peter recognised her face, and his manner softened of a sudden.

"Come awa', lassie, come awa'; a' didna ken ye at the moment, but a' heard ye hed been veesitin' in the sooth.

"The third is terrible full wi' thae Drumtochty lads, and ye 'ill hear naething but Drumsheugh's stirks; ye 'ill maybe be as handy in oor second." And Flora Campbell stepped in unseen.

Between the Junction and Kildrummie Peter was accustomed to wander along the footboard, collecting tickets and identifying passengers. He was generally in fine trim on the way up, and took ample revenge for the insults of the departure. But it was supposed that Peter had taken Drumsheugh's withering sarcasm to heart, for he attached himself to the second that night, and was invisible to the expectant third till the last moment.

"Ye've hed a lang journey, Miss Cammil, and ye maun be nearly dune wi' tire; juist ye sit still till the fouk get awa', and the guid wife and me wud be prood if ye took a cup o' tea wi's afore ye stairted hame. A'll come for ye as sune as a' get the van emptied and ma little trokes feenished."

Peter hurried up to his cottage in such hot haste that his wife came out in great alarm.

"Na, their's naethin' wrang; it's the opposite way this nicht. Ye mind o' Flora Cammil that left her father, and name o' the Drumtochty fouk wud say onything aboot her. Weel, she's in the train, and a've asked her up tae rest, and she was gled tae come, puir thing. Sae gie her a couthy welcome, wumman, and the best in the hoose, for oors 'ill be the first roof she 'ill be under on her way hame."

Our women do not kiss one another like the city ladies; but the motherly grip of Mary Bruce's hand sent a thrill to Flora's heart.

"Noo a' ca' this rael kind o' ye, Miss Cammil, tae come in withoot ceremony, and a'd be terrible pleased if ye would dae it ony time yer traivellin'. The rail is by ordinar' fateegin', and a cup o' tea 'ill set ye up," and Mary had Flora in the best chair, and was loading her plate with homely dainties.

Peter would speak of nothing but the new engine that was coming, and was to place the Kildrummie branch beyond ridicule for ever, and on this great event he continued without intermission till he parted with Flora on the edge of the pine woods that divided Drumtochty from Kildrummie.

"Gude nicht tae ye, Miss Cammil, and thank ye again for yir veesit. Bring the auld man wi' ye next time ye're passing, though a'm feared ye've been deived (deafened) wi' the engine."

Flora took Peter's hand, that was callous and rough

Ian Maclaren

with the turning of brakes and the coupling of chains.

"It wass not your new engine you wass thinking about this night, Peter Bruce, but a poor girl that iss in trouble. I hef not the words, but I will be remembering your house, oh yes, as long as I live."

Twice Peter stood on his way home; the first time he slapped his leg and chuckled:

"Sall, it was gey clever o' me; a hale kerridge o' Drumtochty lads, and no ane o' them ever hed a glint o' her."

At the second stoppage he drew his hand across his eyes.

"Puir lassie, a' houp her father 'ill be kind tae her, for she's sair broken, and looks liker deith than life."

No one can desire a sweeter walk than through a Scottish pine wood in late September, where you breathe the healing resinous air, and the ground is crisp and springy beneath your feet, and gentle animals dart away on every side, and here and there you come on an open space with a pool, and a brake of gorse. Many a time on market days Flora had gone singing through these woods, plucking a posy of wild flowers and finding a mirror in every pool, as young girls will; but now she trembled and was afraid. The rustling of the trees in the darkness, the hooting of an owl, the awful purity of the moonlight in the glades, the cold sheen of the water, were to her troubled conscience omens of judgment. Had it not been for the kindness of Peter Bruce, which was a pledge of human forgiveness, there would have been no heart in her to dare that wood, and it was with a sob of relief she escaped from the shadow and looked upon the old glen once more, bathed from end to end in the light of the harvest moon. Beneath her ran our little river, spanned by its quaint old bridge; away on the right the Parish Kirk peeped out from a clump of trees; half way up the glen the clachan lay surrounded by patches of corn; and beyond were the moors, with a shepherd's cottage that held her heart. Two hours ago squares of light told of warmth and welcome within; but now, as Flora passed one house after another, it seemed as if every one she knew was dead, and she was forgotten in her misery. Her heart grew cold, and she longed to lie down and die, when she caught the gleam of a lighted window. Some one was living still to know she had repented, and she knelt down among the flowers with her ear to the glass to hear the sound of a human voice. Archie Moncur had come home late from a far-away job, but he must needs have worship with his sister before they went to bed, and well did he choose the psalm that night. Flora's tears rained upon the mignonette as the two old people sang:

"When Sion's bondage God turned back,
As men that dreamed were we,
Then filled with laughter was our mouth,
Our tongue with melody;"

while the fragrance of the flowers went up as incense unto God.

All the way along the glen the last words of the psalm still rang in her ears, "Rejoicing shall return," but as she touched the footpath to her home, courage failed her. Marget had written for her dead mother, but no one could speak with authority for her father. She

Ian Maclaren

knew the pride of his religion and his iron principles. If he refused her entrance, then it had been better for her to have died in London. A turn of the path brought her within sight of the cottage, and her heart came into her mouth, for the kitchen window was a blaze of light. One moment she feared Lachlan might be ill, but in the next she understood, and in the greatness of her joy she ran the rest of the way. When she reached the door, her strength had departed, and she was not able to knock. But there was no need, for the dogs, who never forget nor cast off, were bidding her welcome with short joyous yelps of delight, and she could hear her father feeling for the latch, which for once could not be found, and saying nothing but "Flora, Flora."

She had made up some kind of speech, but the only word she ever said was "Father," for Lachlan, who had never even kissed her all the days of her youth, clasped her in his arms and sobbed out blessings over her head, while the dogs licked her hands with their soft, kindly tongues.

"It iss a peety you hef not the Gaelic," Flora said to Marget afterwards; "it iss the best of all languages for loving. There are fifty words for darling, and my father would be calling me every one that night I came home."

Lachlan was so carried with joy, and firelight is so hopeful, that he had not seen the signs of sore sickness on Flora's face, but the morning light undeceived him, and he was sadly dashed.

"You will be fery tired after your long journey, Flora, and it iss good for you to rest. There iss a man in the clachan I am wanting to see, and he will maybe be comin' back with me."

When Lachlan reached his place of prayer, he lay on the ground and cried, "Have mercy on me, O Lord, and spare her for Thy servant's sake, and let me not lose her after Thou hast brought her back and hast opened my heart.... Take her not till she hass seen that I love her.... Give me time to do her kindness for the past wherein I oppressed her.... O, turn away Thy judgment on my hardness, and let not the child suffer for her father's sins." Then he arose and hastened for the doctor.

It was afternoon before Dr. MacLure could come, but the very sight of his face, which was as the sun in its strength, let light into the room where Lachlan sat at the bedside holding Flora's hand, and making woful pretence that she was not ill.

"Weel, Flora, yeve got back frae yir veesits, and a' tell ye we've a' missed ye maist terrible. A' doot thae sooth country fouk haena been feeding ye ower weel, or maybe it was the toon air. It never agrees wi' me. A'm half chokit a' the time a'm in Glesgie, and as for London, there's ower mony fouk tae the square yaird for health."

All the time he was busy at his work, and no man could do it better or quicker, although the outside of him was not encouraging.

"Lachlan, what are ye traivellin' in and oot there for with a face that wud sour milk? What ails ye, man? ye're surely no imaginin' Flora's gaein' to leave ye?

"Lord's sake, it's maist provokin' that if a body hes a bit

Ian Maclaren

whup o' illness in Drumtochty, their freends tak tae propheseein' deith."

Lachlan had crept over to Flora's side, and both were waiting.

"Na, na; ye ken a' never tell lees like the graund ceety doctors, and a'll warrant Flora 'ill be in kirk afore Martinmas, an' kiltin' up the braes as hardy as a hielan' sheltie by the new year."

Flora puts an arm round her father's neck, and draws down his face to hers, but the doctor is looking another way.

"Dinna fash wi' medicine; gie her plenty o' fresh milk and plenty o' air. There's nae leevin' for a doctor wi' that Drumtochty air; it hasna a marra in Scotland. It starts frae the Moray Firth and sweeps doon Badenoch, and comes ower the moor o' Rannoch and across the Grampians. There's the salt o' the sea, and the caller air o' the hills, and the smell o' the heather, and the bloom o'mony a flower in't. If there's nae disease in the organs o' the body, a puff o' Drumtochty air wud bring back a man frae the gates o' deith."

"You hef made two hearts glad this day, Doctor McLure," said Lachlan, outside the door, "and I am calling you Barnabas."

"Ye've ca'd me waur names than that in yir time," and the doctor mounted his horse. "It's dune me a warld o' guid tae see Flora in her hame again, and I'll gie Marget Howe a cry in passin' and send her up tae hae a crack, for there's no a wiser wumman in the glen."

When Marget came, Flora told her the history of her letter.

"It wass a beautiful night in London, but I will be thinking that there iss no living person caring whether I die or live, and I wass considering how I could die, for there iss nothing so hopeless as to hef no friend in a great city. It iss often that I hef been alone on the moor, and no man within miles, but I wass never lonely, oh no, I had plenty of good company. I would sit down beside a burn, and the trout will swim out from below a stone, and the cattle will come to drink, and the muirfowl will be crying to each other, and the sheep will be bleating, oh yes, and there are the bees all round, and a string of wild ducks above your head. It iss a busy place a moor, and a safe place too, for there iss not one of the animals will hurt you. No, the big highlanders will only look at you and go away to their pasture. But it iss weary to be in London and no one to speak a kind word to you, and I will be looking at the crowd that iss always passing, and I will not see one kent face, and when I looked in at the lighted windows the people were all sitting round the table, but there wass no place for me. Millions and millions of people, and not one to say 'Flora,' and not one sore heart if I died that night. Then a strange thing happened, as you will be considering, but it iss good to be a Highlander, for we see visions. You maybe know that a wounded deer will try to hide herself, and I crept into the shadow of a church, and wept. Then the people and the noise and the houses passed away like the mist on the hill, and I wass walking to the kirk with my father, oh yes, and I saw you all in your places, and I heard the Psalms, and I could see through the window the green fields and the trees on the edge of the moor. And I saw my home,

Ian Maclaren

with the dogs before the door, and the flowers that I planted, and the lamb coming for her mik, and I heard myself singing, and I awoke. But there wass singing, oh yes, and beautiful too, for the dark church wass open, and the light wass falling over my head from the face of the Virgin Mary. When I arose she wass looking down at me in the darkness, and then I knew that there wass service in the church, and this wass the hymn -

"'There is a fountain filled with blood.'

"So I went in and sat down at the door. The sermon wass on the Prodigal Son, but there iss only one word I remember. 'You are not forgotten or cast off,' the preacher said; 'you are missed,' and then he will come back to it again, and it wass always 'missed, missed, missed.' Sometimes he will say, 'If you had a plant, and you had taken great care of it, and it was stolen, would you not miss it?' And I will be thinking of my geraniums, and saying 'yes' in my heart. And then he will go on, 'If a shepherd wass counting his sheep, and there wass one short, does he not go out to the hill and seek for it?' and I will see my father coming back with that lamb that lost its mother. My heart wass melting within me, but he will still be pleading, 'If a father had a child, and she left her home and lost herself in the wicked city, she will still be remembered in the old house, and her chair will be there,' and I will be seeing my father all alone with the Bible before him, and the dogs will lay their heads on his knee, but there iss no Flora. So I slipped out into the darkness and cried 'Father,' but I could not go back, and I knew not what to do. But this wass ever in my ear, 'missed,' and I wass wondering if God will be thinking of me. 'Perhaps there may be a sign,' I said, and I went to my room, and I saw the letter. It wass not long before I will be in the train, and all the night I held your letter in my hand, and when I wass afraid I will read 'Your father loves you more than efer,' and I will say, 'This is my warrant.' Oh yes, and God wass very good to me, and I did not want for friends all the way home.

"The English guard noticed me cry, and he will take care of me all the night, and see me off at Muirtown, and this iss what he will say as the train wass leaving, in his cheery English way, 'Keep up your heart, lass, there's a good time coming,' and Peter Bruce will be waiting for me at the Junction, and a gentle man iss Peter Bruce, and Maister Moncur will be singing a psalm to keep up my heart, and I will see the light, and then I will know that the Lord hass had mercy upon me. That iss all I have to tell you, Marget, for the rest I will be saying to God."

"But there iss something I must be telling," said Lachlan, coming in, "and it iss not easy."

He brought over the Bible and opened it at the family register where his daughter's name had been erased; then he laid it down before Flora, and bowed his head on the bed.

"Will you ever be able to forgive your father?"

"Give me the pen, Marget;" and Flora wrote for a minute, but Lachlan never moved.

When he lifted his head, this was what he read in a vacant space: -

Ian Maclaren

FLORA CAMPBELL.
Missed April 1873.
Found September 1873.
"Her father fell on her neck and kissed her."

IV

AS A LITTLE CHILD

Drumtochty made up its mind slowly upon any new-comer, and for some time looked into the far distance when his name was mentioned. He himself was struck with the studied indifference of the parish, and lived under the delusion that he had escaped notice. Perhaps he might have felt uncomfortable if he had suspected that he was under a microscope, and the keenest eyes in the country were watching every movement at kirk and market. His knowledge of theology, his preference in artificial manures, his wife's Sabbath dress, his skill in cattle, and his manner in the Kildrummie train, went as evidence in the case, and were duly weighed. Some morning the floating opinion suddenly crystallized in the kirkyard, and there is only one historical instance in which judgment was reversed. It was a strong proof of Lachlan Campbell's individuality that he impressed himself twice on the parish, and each time with a marked adjective.

Lachlan had been superintending the theology of the glen and correcting our ignorance from an unapproachable height for two years before the word went forth, but the glen had been thinking.

"Lachlan is a carefu' shepherd and fine wi' the ewes at

Ian Maclaren

the lambing time, there's nae doot o' that, but a' canna thole (bear) himsel'. Ye wud think there was nae releegion in the parish till he came frae Auchindarroch. What say ye, Domsie?"

"Campbell's a censorious body, Drumsheugh," and Domsie shut his snuff-box lid with a snap.

Drumsheugh nodded to the fathers of our common-wealth, and they went into kirk with silent satisfaction. Lachlan had been classified, and Peter Bruce, who prided himself on keeping in touch with Drumtochty, passed the word round the Kildrummie train next market night.

"Ye haena that censorious body, Lachlan Campbell, wi' ye the nicht," thrusting his head in on the thirds.

"There's naething Peter disna ken," Hillocks remarked with admiration afterwards; "he's as gude as the *Advertiser*."

When Flora had come home, and Drumtochty resumed freedom of criticism, I noticed for the first time a certain vacillation in its treatment of Lachlan.

"He's pluckit up his speerit maist extraordinar," Hillocks explained, "and he whuppit by me like a three year auld laist Sabbath.

"'I'm glad tae hear the Miss is comin' roond fine,' says I.

"'It's the fouk o' Drumtochty hes made her weel. God bless you, for you hev done good for evil,' and wi' that he was aff afore I cud fin' a word.

"He's changed, the body, some wy or ither, and there's a kind o' warmth aboot him ye canna get ower."

Next day I turned into Mrs. Macfadyen's cottage for a cup of tea and the smack of that wise woman's conversation, but was not able to pass the inner door for the sight which met my eyes.

Lachlan was sitting on a chair in the middle of the kitchen with Elsie, Mrs. Macfadyen's pet child, on his knee, and their heads so close together that his white hair was mingling with her burnished gold. An odour of peppermint floated out at the door, and Elsie was explaining to Lachlan, for his guidance at the shop, that the round drops were a better bargain than the black and white rock.

When Lachlan had departed, with gracious words on his lips and a very sticky imprint on his right cheek, I settled down in the big chair, beyond the power of speech, and Mrs. Macfadyen opened the mystery.

"Ye may weel look, for twa month syne I wudna hae believed this day, though a' hed seen him wi' ma ain een.

"It was juist this time laist year that he cam here on his elder's veesitation, and he catches the bairn in this verra kitchen.

"'Elspeth,' says he - it was Elsie the day, ye mind - 'div ye ken that ye're an oreeginal sinner?'

"It was nichtfa' afore she got over the fricht, and when she saw him on the road next Sabbath, she cooried in ahint ma goon, and cried till I thocht her hert wud break.

"'It's meeserable wark for Christ's Elder,' says Jeems, 'tae put the fear o' death on a bairn, and a'm thinkin' he wudna get muckle thanks frae his Maister if He wes here,' and Jeems wasna far wrong, though, of course, a' told him tae keep a quiet sough, and no conter the elder.

"Weel, I sees Lachlan comin' up the road the day, and a' ran oot to catch Elsie and hide her in the byre. But a' micht hae saved mysel' the trouble: afore I got tae the gairden gate they were comin' up as chief (friendly) as ye like, and Lachlan wes callin' Elsie his bonnie dawtie.

"If he hadna a pock o' peppermints - but it wesna that wiled Elsie's hert. Na, na, dogs and bairns can read fouks' faces, and mak nae mistakes. As sune as a' saw Lachlan's een a' kent he wes a new man.

"Hoo has it come about? That's easy tae guess. Sax months syne Lachlan didna ken what father meant, and the heart wes wizened in the breist o' him wi' pride an' diveenity.

"He kens noo, and a'm jalousing that nae man can be a richt father tae his ain without being sib (akin) tae every bairn he sees. It wes Flora he was dawting (petting) ye see the day, and he's learned his trade weel, though it cost him a sair lesson."

Wonderful stories circulated through the glen, and were told in the kirkyard of a Sabbath morning, concerning the transformation of Lachlan Campbell.

"Ane o' ma wee lassies," expatiated Domsie, "fell comin' doon the near road frae Whinnie Knowe, and cuttit her cheek on the stones, and if Lachlan didna wash her face and comfort her; an' mair, he carried her a' the road tae the schule, and says he in his Hieland way, 'Here iss a brave little woman that hass hurt herself, but she will not be crying,' and he gave her a kiss and a penny tae buy some sweeties at the shop. It minded me o' the Gude Samaritan, fouks," and everybody understood that Lachlan had captured Domsie for life.

"It beats a' things," said Whinnie; "a' canna mak' oot what's come ower the cratur. There's a puckle o' the upland bairns pass oor wy frae schule, and whiles Lachlan 'ill meet them when he's aifter his sheep, and as sure as a'm stannin' here, he 'ill lay aff stories aboot battles and fairies, till the laddies 'ill hardly gae hame. I wes tellin' Marget this verra mornin', and she says, 'Lachlan's become as a little child.' I dinna haud wi' her there, but a quieter, mair cautious body ye never saw."

Drumtochty was doing its best to focus Lachlan afresh, and felt the responsibility lay on Domsie, who accepted it cheerfully.

"Marget's aye richt, neebours, and she's put the word on it noo. His tribble hes melted Lachlan's heart, an' - it's in the Evangel, ye ken - he's become as a little child."

This language was too figurative and imposing for the parish, but it ran henceforward in our modest speech, "He's a cautious body." Cautious, with us, meant unassuming, kindly obliging, as well as much more; and I still hear Drumsheugh pronouncing this final judgment of the glen on Lachlan as we parted at his grave ten years later, and adding, "He 'ill be sair missed by the bairns."

While the glen was readjusting itself to Lachlan, I came down from a long tramp on the moor, and intended to inquire for Flora. But I was arrested on the step by the sound of Lachlan's voice in family worship.

"This my son was dead, and is alive again; he was lost, and is found. And they began to be merry."

Lachlan's voice trembled as he read, but he went on with much firmness:

"Now his elder son was in the field."

"You will not be reading more of that chapter, father," interrupted Flora, with a new note of authority.

"And why not?" said Lachlan, quite humbly.

"Because you will be calling yourself the elder son and many more bad names, and I will be angry with you."

"But they are true names, and it iss good for me to know myself."

"You hef just one true name, and that iss father.... And now you will be singing a psalm."

"There iss a book of himes (hymns) here, and maybe you will be liking one of them."

And Lachlan produced the little book Flora got in that London church when the preacher told her she was missed.

"We will not sing hymns, father, for I am remembering that you hef a conscience against hymns, and I did not know that you had that book."

"My conscience wass sometimes better than the Bible, Flora, and if God will be sending a hime to bind up your heart when it wass broken, it iss your father that will be wanting to sing that hime.

"It iss here," continued Lachlan in triumph, "for I hef often been reading that hime, and I am not seeing much wrong in it."

"But each hymn hass got its own tune, father, and you will not know the way that it goes, and the doctor will not be wishing me to sing."

"You are a good girl, Flora, but you are not so clever as your father, oh no, for I hef been trying that hime on the hill, and it will sing beautiful to a Psalm tune. You will lie still and hear."

Then Lachlan lifted up his voice in "French,"

"There is a fountain filled with blood,
Drawn from Immanuel's veins,
And sinners plunged beneath that flood
Lose all their guilty stains."

The singing was fairly good, with a whisper from Flora, till they came to that verse:

"Then in a nobler, sweeter song
I'll sing Thy power to save,

When this poor lisping, stammering tongue
Lies silent in the grave,"

when Lachlan seemed to lose the tune, and be falling into a coronach.

"We must not be singing that to-day, father, for God iss fery good to us, and I will be stronger every week, and maybe you will be saying that we are thankful in your prayer."

Then I realised my baseness, and went off on tiptoe (had the dogs been at home it had not been so easy to escape); but first I heard, "Our Father." It was a new word for Lachlan; he used to say Jehovah.

The doctor paid his last visit one frosty winter day, and was merciless on Lachlan.

"What for are ye cockering up this lassie, and no getting her doon tae the kirk? it's clean disgracefu' in an Elder, and if I were yir minister a' wud hae ye sessioned. Sall, ye're hard enough on ither fouk that are no kirk greedy."

"You will not be speaking that way next Sabbath, for it iss in her pew Flora will be sitting with her father," said Lachlan, in great spirits.

Flora caught him studying her closely for some days, as if he were taking her measure, and he announced that he had business in Muirtown on Friday.

When he came up in the market train he was carrying a large paper parcel, and attempted a joke with Peter at a window of the third. From a critical point of view it was beneath notice, but as Lachlan's first effort it was much tasted.

"Ye 'ill believe me noo, Peter, since ye've heard him. Did ye ever see sic a change? it's maist astonishin'."

"Man, Hillocks, div ye no see he's gotten back his dochter, and it's made him anither man?"

Lachlan showed Flora a new pair of shears he had bought in Muirtown, and a bottle of sheep embrocation, but she did not know he had hidden his parcel in the byre, and that he opened it four separate times on Saturday.

From daybreak on Sabbath Lachlan went in and out till he returned with Marget Howe.

"Mrs. Howe iss very kind, and she will be coming to help you with your dresses, Flora, for we will be wanting you to look well this day, and here iss some small thing to keep you warm," and Lachlan produced with unspeakable pride a jacket lined with flannel and trimmed with fur.

So her father and Marget dressed Flora for the kirk, and they went together down the path on which the light had shone that night of her return.

There were only two dog-carts in the Free Kirk Session, and Burnbrae was waiting with his for Flora at the foot of the hill.

"I bid ye welcome, Flora, in the name o' oor kirk. It's a gled day for your father, and for us a' tae see you back again and strong. And noo ye 'ill just get up aside me

Ian Maclaren

in the front, and Mistress Hoo 'ill hap ye round, for we maunna let ye come tae ony ill the first day yir oot, or we 'ill never hear the end o't." And so the honest man went on, for he was as near the breaking as Drumtochty nature allowed.

"A' body's pleased," said Marget to Lachlan as they sat on the back seat and caught the faces of the people. "This is the first time I have seen the fifteenth of Luke in Drumtochty. It's a bonnie sicht, and a'm thinkin' it's still bonnier in the presence o' the angels."

"Flora Cammil's in the kirk the day," and the precentor looked at Carmichael with expectation. "The fouk are terrible taen up wi' Lachlan and her."

"What do you think of the hundred and third Psalm, Robert? It would go well this morning."

"The verra word that was on my lips, and Lachlan 'ill be lookin' for Coleshill."

Lachlan had put Flora in his old place next the wall (he would not need it again, having retired from the office of inquisitor), and sat close beside her, with great contentment on his face. The manners of Drumtochty were perfect, and no one turned his head by one inch; but Marget Howe, sitting behind in Burnbrae's pew, saw Flora's hand go out to Lachlan's as the people sang:

> "All thine iniquities who doth
> Most graciously forgive,
> Who thy diseases all and pains
> Doth heal and thee relieve."

The Session met that week, and a young girl broke down utterly in her examination for the Sacrament, so that not even Burnbrae could get a correct answer.

She rose in great confusion and sorrow.

"A' see it wudna be fit for the like o' me tae gae forrit, but a' had set ma hert on't; it wes the last thing He askit o' His freends," and she left before any one could bid her stay.

"Moderator," said Lachlan, "it iss a great joy for me to move that Mary Macfarlane get her token, and I will be wishing that we all had her warrant, oh yes, for there iss no warrant like love. And there iss something that I must be asking of the elders, and it iss to forgive me for my pride in this Session. I wass thinking that I knew more than any man in Drumtochty, and wass judging God's people. But He hass had mercy upon Simon the Pharisee, and you hef all been been very good to me and Flora.... The Scripture hass been fulfilled, 'So the last shall be first, and the first last.'"

Then the minister asked Burnbrae to pray, and the Spirit descended on that good man, of simple heart:

"Almichty Father, we are a' Thy puir and sinfu' bairns, wha wearied o' hame and gaed awa' intae the far country. Forgive us, for we didna ken what we were leavin' or the sair hert we gied oor Father. It wes weary wark tae live wi' oor sins, but we wud never hev come back had it no been for oor Elder Brither. He cam' a long road tae find us, and a sore travail He had afore He set us free. He's been a gude Brither tae us, and we've been a heavy chairge tae Him. May He keep a firm haud o' us, and guide us in the richt road, and

Ian Maclaren

bring us back gin we wander, and tell us a' we need tae know till the gloamin' come. Gither us in then, we pray Thee, and a' we luve, no a bairn missin', and may we sit doon for ever in oor ain Father's House. Amen."

* * * * *

As Burnbrae said Amen, Carmichael opened his eyes, and had a vision which will remain with him until the day break and the shadows flee away.

The six elders - three small farmers, a tailor, a stonemason, and a shepherd - were standing beneath the lamp, and the light fell like a halo on their bent heads. That poor little vestry had disappeared, and this present world was forgotten. The sons of God had come into their heritage, "for the things which are seen are temporal, but the things which are not seen are eternal."

THE CUNNING SPEECH OF DRUMTOCHTY

Speech in Drumtochty distilled slowly, drop by drop, and the faces of our men were carved in stone. Visitors, without discernment, used to pity our dulness and lay themselves out for missionary work. Before their month was over they spoke bitterly of us, as if we had deceived them, and departed with a grudge in their hearts. When Hillocks scandalised the Glen by letting his house and living in the bothie - through sheer greed of money - it was taken by a fussy little man from the South, whose control over the letter "h" was uncertain, but whose self-confidence bordered on the miraculous. As a deacon of the Social Religionists, - a new denomination, which had made an 'it with Sunday Entertainments, - and Chairman of the Amalgamated Sons of Rest, - a society of persons with conscientious objections to work between meals - he was horrified at the primeval simplicity of the Glen, where no meeting of protest had been held in the memory of living man, and the ministers preached from the Bible. It was understood that he was to do his best for us, and there was curiosity in the kirkyard.

"Whatna like man is that English veesitor ye've got, Hillocks? a' hear he's fleein' ower the Glen, yammerin' and haverin' like a starlin'."

"He's a gabby (talkative) body, Drumsheugh, there's

Ian Maclaren

nae doot o' that, but terrible ignorant.

"Says he tae me nae later than yesterday, 'That's a fine field o' barley ye've there, Maister Harris,' an' as sure as deith a' didna ken whaur tae luik, for it was a puckle aits."

"Keep's a'," said Whinnie; "he's been awfu' negleckit when he wes a bairn, or maybe there's a want in the puir cratur."

Next Sabbath Mr. Urijah Hopps appeared in person among the fathers - who looked at each other over his head - and enlightened them on supply and demand, the Game Laws, the production of cabbages for towns, the iniquity of an Established Church, and the bad metre of the Psalms of David.

"You must 'ave henterprise, or it's hall hup with you farmers."

"Ay, ay," responded Drumsheugh, after a long pause, and then every man concentrated his attention on the belfry of the kirk.

"Is there onything ava' in the body, think ye, Domsie," as Mr. Hopps bustled into kirk, "or is't a' wind?"

"Three wechtfu's o' naething, Drumsheugh; a' peety the puir man if Jamie Soutar gets a haud o' him."

Jamie was the cynic of the Glen - who had pricked many a wind bag - and there was a general feeling that his meeting with Mr. Hopps would not be devoid of interest. When he showed himself anxious to learn next Sabbath, any man outside Drumtochty might have been deceived, for Jamie could withdraw every sign of intelligence from his face, as when shutters close upon a shop window. Our visitor fell at once into the trap, and made things plain to the meanest capacity, until Jamie elicited from the guileless Southron that he had never heard of the Act of Union; that Adam Smith was a new book he hoped to buy; that he did not know the difference between an Arminian and a Calvinist, and that he supposed the Confession of Faith was invented in Edinburgh. This in the briefest space of time, and by way of information to Drumtochty. James was making for general literature, and had still agriculture in reserve, when Drumsheugh intervened in the humanity of his heart.

"A' dinna like tae interrupt yir conversation, Maister Hopps, but it's no verra safe for ye tae be stannin' here sae lang. Oor air hes a bit nip in't, and is mair searchin' than doon Sooth. Jamie 'ill be speirin' a' mornin' gin ye 'ill answer him, but a'm thinkin' ye'ill be warmer in the kirk."

And Drumsheugh escorted Mr. Hopps to cover, who began to suspect that he had been turned inside out, and found wanting.

Drumtochty had listened with huge delight, but without a trace of expression, and, on Mr. Hopps reaching shelter, three boxes were offered Jamie.

The group was still lost in admiration when Drumsheugh returned from his errand of mercy.

"Sall, ye've dune the job this time. Jamie. Ye're an awfu' creetic. Yon man 'ill keep a quiet cheep till he gets Sooth. It passes me hoo a body wi' sae little in him

128   Ian Maclaren

hes the face tae open his mooth."

"Ye did it weel, Jamie," Domsie added, "a clean furrow frae end tae end."

"Toots, fouk, yir makin' ower muckle o' it. It wes licht grund, no worth puttin' in a ploo."

Mr. Hopps explained to me, before leaving, that he had been much pleased with the scenery of our Glen, but disappointed in the people.

"They may not be hignorant," said the little man doubtfully, "but no man could call them haffable."

It flashed on me for the first time that perhaps there may have been the faintest want of geniality in the Drumtochty manner, but it was simply the reticence of a subtle and conscientious people. Intellect with us had been brought to so fine an edge by the Shorter Catechism that it could detect endless distinctions, and was ever on the watch against inaccuracy. Farmers who could state the esoteric doctrine of "spiritual independence" between the stilts of the plough, and talked familiarly of "co-ordinate jurisdiction with mutual subordination," were not likely to fall into the vice of generalisation. When James Soutar was in good fettle, he could trace the whole history of Scottish secession from the beginning, winding his way through the maze of Original Seceders and Cameronians, Burghers and Anti-Burghers - there were days when he would include the Glassites, - with unfaltering step; but this was considered a feat even in Drumtochty, and it was admitted that Jamie had "a gift o' discreemination." We all had the gift in measure, and dared not therefore allow ourselves the expansive language of the South. What right had any human being to fling about superlative adjectives, seeing what a big place the world is, and how little we know? Purple adjectives would have been as much out of place in our conversation as a bird of paradise among our muirfowl.

Mr. Hopps was so inspired by one of our sunsets - to his credit let that be told - that he tried to drive Jamie into extravagance.

"No bad! I call it glorious, and if it hisn't, then I'd like to know what his."

"Man," replied Soutar austerely, "ye 'ill surely keep ae word for the twenty-first o' Reevelation."

Had any native used "magnificent," there would have been an uneasy feeling in the Glen; the man must be suffering from wind in the head, and might upset the rotation of crops, sowing his young grass after potatoes, or replacing turnip with beetroot. But nothing of that sort happened in my time; we kept ourselves well in hand. It rained in torrents elsewhere, with us it only "threatened tae be weet" - some provision had to be made for the deluge. Strangers, in the pride of health, described themselves as "fit for anything," but Hillocks, who died at ninety-two, and never had an hour's illness, did not venture, in his prime, beyond "Gaein' aboot, a'm thankfu' to say, gaein' aboot."

When one was seriously ill, he was said to be "gey an' sober," and no one died in Drumtochty - "he slippit awa."

Hell and heaven were pulpit words; in private life we spoke of "the ill place" and "oor lang hame."

When the corn sprouted in the stooks one late wet harvest, and Burnbrae lost half his capital, he only said, "It's no lichtsome," and no congratulations on a good harvest ever extracted more from Drumsheugh than "A' daurna complain."

Drumsheugh might be led beyond bounds in reviewing a certain potato transaction, but, as a rule, he was a master of measured speech. After the privilege of much intercourse with that excellent man, I was able to draw up his table of equivalents for the three degrees of wickedness. When there was just a suspicion of trickiness - neglecting the paling between your cattle and your neighbour's clover field - "He's no juist the man for an elder." If it deepened into deceit - running a "greasy" horse for an hour before selling - "He wud be the better o' anither dip." And in the case of downright fraud - finding out what a man had offered for his farm and taking it over his head - the offender was "an ill gettit wratch." The two latter phrases were dark with theology, and even the positive degree of condemnation had an ecclesiastical flavour.

When Drumsheugh approved any one, he was content to say, "He micht be waur," a position beyond argument. On occasion he ventured upon bolder assertions: "There's nae mischief in Domsie;" and once I heard him in a white heat of enthusiasm pronounce Dr. Davidson, our parish minister, "A graund man ony wy ye tak him." But he seemed ashamed after this outburst, and "shooed" the crows off the corn with needless vigour.

No Drumtochty man would commit himself to a positive statement on any subject if he could find a way of escape, not because his mind was confused, but because he was usually in despair for an accurate expression. It was told for years in the Glen, with much relish and almost funereal solemnity, how a Drumtochty witness had held his own in an ecclesiastical court.

"You are beadle in the parish of Pitscouric," began the advocate with a light heart, not knowing the witness's birthplace.

"It's a fac'," after a long pause and a careful review of the whole situation.

"You remember that Sabbath when the minister of Netheraird preached."

"Weel, a'll admit that," making a concession to justice.

"Did ye see him in the vestry?"

"A' canna deny it."

"Was he intoxicated?"

The crudeness of this question took away Drumtochty's breath, and suggested that something must have been left out in the creation of that advocate. Our men were not bigoted abstainers, but I never heard any word so coarse and elementary as intoxicated used in Drumtochty. Conversation touched this kind of circumstance with delicacy and caution, for we keenly realised the limitations of human knowledge.

"He hed his mornin'," served all ordinary purposes, and in cases of emergency, such as Muirtown market:

"Ye cud see he hed been tastin'."

When an advocate forgot himself so far as to say intoxicated, a Drumtochty man might be excused for being upset.

"Losh, man," when he had recovered, "hoo cud ony richt-thinkin' man sweer tae sic an awfu' word? Na, na, a' daurna use that kin' o' langidge; it's no cannie."

The advocate tried again, a humbler, wiser man.

"Was there a smell of drink on him?"

"Noo, since ye press me, a'll juist tell ye the hale truth; it wes doonricht stupid o' me, but, as sure as a'm livin', a' clean forgot tae try him."

Then the chastened counsel gathered himself up for his last effort.

"Will you answer one question, sir? you are on your oath. Did you see anything unusual in Mr. MacOmish's walk? Did he stagger?"

"Na," when he had spent two minutes in recalling the scene. "Na, I cudna say stagger, but he micht gie a bit trimmil."

"We are coming to the truth now; what did you consider the cause of the trimmiling, as you call it?" and the innocent young advocate looked round in triumph.

"Weel," replied Drumtochty, making a clean breast of it, "since ye maun hae it, a' heard that he wes a very learned man, and it cam intae ma mind that the Hebrew, which, a'm telt, is a very contrairy langidge, hed gaen doon and settled in his legs."

The parish of Netheraird was declared vacant, but it was understood that the beadle of Pitscourie had not contributed to this decision.

His own parish followed the trial with intense interest, and were much pleased with Andra's appearance.

"Sall," said Hillocks, "Andra has mair gumption than ye wud think, and yon advocat didna mak muckle o' him. Na, na, Andra wesna brocht up in the Glen for naethin'. Maister MacOmish may hae taen his gless atween the Hebrew and the Greek, and it's no verra suitable for a minister, but that's anither thing frae bein' intoxicat."

"Keep's a', if ye were tae pit me in the box this meenut, a' cudna sweer a hed ever seen a man intoxicat in ma life, except a puir body o' an English bag-man at Muirtown Station. A' doot he hed bin meddlin' wi' speerits, and they were wheelin' him tae his kerridge in a luggage barrow. It wes a fearsome sicht, and eneugh tae keep ony man frae speakin' aboot intoxicat in yon louse wy."

Archie Moncur fought the drinking customs of the Glen night and day with moderate success, and one winter's night he gave me a study in his subject which, after the lapse of years, I still think admirable for its reserve power and Dantesque conclusion.

"They a' begin in a sma' wy," explained Archie, almost hidden in the depths of my reading chair, and emphasising his points with a gentle motion of his right hand; "naethin' tae mention at first, juist a gless at an orra time - a beerial or a merridge - and maybe New Year. That's the first stage; they ca' that moderation. Aifter a whilie they tak a mornin' wi' a freend, and syne a gless at the public-hoose in the evenin', and they treat ane anither on market days. That's the second stage; that's 'tastin'.' Then they need it reg'lar every day, nicht an' mornin', and they'll sit on at nicht till they're turned oot. They 'ill fecht ower the Confession noo, and laist Sabbath's sermon, in the Kildrummie train, till it's clean reediklus. That's drammin', and when they've hed a year or twa at that they hae their first spatie (spate is a river flood), and that gies them a bit fricht. But aff they set again, and then comes anither spatie, and the doctor hes tae bring them roond. They ca' (drive) cannie for a year or sae, but the feein' market puts the feenishin' titch. They slip aff sudden in the end, and then they juist gang plunk - ay," said Archie in a tone of gentle meditation, looking, as it were, over the edge, "juist plunk."

Nothing ever affected my imagination more power-fully than the swift surprise and gruesome suggestion of that "plunk."

But the literary credit of Drumtochty rested on a broad basis, and no one could live with us without having his speech braced for life. You felt equal to any emergency, and were always able to express your mind with some degree of accuracy, which is one of the luxuries of life. There is, for instance, a type of idler who exasperates one to the point of assault, and whom one hungers to describe after a becoming manner. He was rare in the cold air of the North, but we had produced one specimen, and it was my luck to be present when he came back from a distant colony, and Jamie Soutar welcomed him in the kirkyard.

"Weel, Chairlie," and Jamie examined the well-dressed prodigal from top to toe, "this is a prood moment for Drumtochty, and an awfu' relief tae ken yir safe. Man, ye hevna wanted meat nor claithes; a' tak it rael neeburly o' ye tae speak ava wi' us auld-fashioned fouk.

"Ye needna look soor nor cock yir nose in the air, for you an' me are auld freends, and yir puir granny wes na mair anxious aboot ye than a' wes.

"A'm feared that laddie o' Bell's 'ill kill himsel' oot in Ameriky' were ma verra words tae Hillocks here; 'he 'ill be slavin' his flesh aff his banes tae mak a fortune and keep her comfortable'

"It was a rael satisfaction tae read yir letter frae the backwoods - or was't a public-hoose in New York? ma memory's no what it used to be - tellin' hoo ye were aye thinkin' o' yer auld granny, and wantin' tae come hame and be a comfort tae her if she wud send ye out twenty pund.

"The bit that affeckit me maist wes the text frae the Prodigal Son - it cam in sae natural. Mony a broken hert hes that story bund up, as we ken weel in this Glen; but it's dune a feck o' mischief tae - that gude word o' the Maister. Half the wastrels in the warld pay their passage hame wi' that Parable, and get a bran new outfit for anither start in the far country.

"Noo dinna turn red, Chairlie, for the neeburs ken ye were tae work yir wy hame hed it no been for yir health. But there's a pack of rascals 'ill sorn on their father as lang as he's livin', and they 'ill stairve a weedowed mither, and they 'ill tak a sister's wages, and if they canna get ony better a dune body o' eighty 'ill serve them.

"Man, Chairlie, if a' hed ma wull wi' thae wawfies, I wud ship them aff tae a desert island, wi' ae sack o' seed potatoes and anither o' seed corn, and let them work or dee. A' ken yir wi' me there, for ye aye hed an independent spirit, and wesna feared tae bend yir back.

"Noo, if a' cam across ane o' thae meeserable objects in Drumtochty, div ye ken the advice I wud gie him?

"A wud tell the daidlin', thowless, feckless, fushionless wratch o' a cratur tae watch for the first spate and droon himsel' in the Tochty."

"What's he aff through the graves for in sic a hurry?" and Jamie followed Charlie's retreating figure with a glance of admirable amazement; "thae's no very gude mainners he's learned in Americky."

"Thank ye, Jeemes, thank ye; we're a' obleeged tae ye," said Drumsheugh. "A' wes ettlin' tae lay ma hands on the whup-ma-denty (fop) masel, but ma certes, he's hed his kail het this mornin'. Div ye think he 'ill tak yir advice?"

"Nae fear o' him; thae neer-dae-weels haena the spunk; but a'm expeckin' he 'ill flee the pairish."

Which he did. Had you called him indolent or useless he had smiled, but "daidlin', thowless, feckless, fushionless wratch," drew blood at every stroke, like a

Russian knout.

We had tender words also, that still bring the tears to my eyes, and chief among them was "couthy." What did it mean? It meant a letter to some tired townsman, written in homely Scotch, and bidding him come to get new life from the Drumtochty air; and the grip of an honest hand on the Kildrummie platform whose warmth lasted till you reached the Glen; and another welcome at the garden-gate that mingled with the scent of honeysuckle, and moss-roses, and thyme, and carnations; and the best of everything that could be given you; and motherly nursing in illness, with skilly remedies of the olden time; and wise, cheery talk that spake no ill of man or God; and loud reproaches if you proposed to leave under a month or two; and absolute conditions that you must return; and a load of country dainties for a bachelor's bare commons; and far more, that cannot be put into words, of hospitality, and kindness, and quietness, and restfulness, and loyal friendship of hearts now turned to dust in the old kirkyard.

But the best of all our words were kept for spiritual things, and the description of a godly man. We did not speak of the "higher life," nor of a "beautiful Christian," for this way of putting it would not have been in keeping with the genius of Drumtochty. Religion there was very lowly and modest - an inward walk with God. No man boasted of himself, none told the secrets of the soul. But the Glen took notice of its saints, and did them silent reverence, which they themselves never knew. Jamie Soutar had a wicked tongue, and, at a time, it played round Archie's temperance schemes, but when that good man's back was turned Jamie was the first to do him justice.

Ian Maclaren

"It wud set us better if we did as muckle gude as Archie; he's a richt livin' man and weel prepared."

Our choicest tribute was paid by general consent to Burnbrae, and it may be partiality, but it sounds to me the deepest in religious speech. Every cottage, strangers must understand, had at least two rooms - the kitchen where the work was done, that we called the "But," and there all kinds of people came; and the inner chamber which held the household treasures, that we called the "Ben," and there none but a few honoured visitors had entrance. So we imagined an outer court of the religious life where most of us made our home, and a secret place where only God's nearest friends could enter, and it was said of Burnbrae, "He's far ben." His neighbours had watched him, for a generation and more, buying and selling, ploughing and reaping, going out and in the common ways of a farmer's life, and had not missed the glory of the soul. The cynic of Drumtochty summed up his character: "There's a puckle gude fouk in the pairish, and ane or twa o' the ither kind, and the maist o' us are half and between," said Jamie Soutar, "but there's ae thing ye may be sure o', Burnbrae is 'far ben.'"

A WISE WOMAN

I

OUR SERMON TASTER

A Drumtochty man, standing six feet three in his boots, sat himself down one day in the study of a West-end minister, and gazed before him with the countenance of a sphinx.

The sight struck awe into the townsman's heart, and the power of speech was paralysed within him.

"A'm frae Drumtochty," began a deep solemn voice. "Ye 'ill hae heard of Drumtochty, of coorse. A've jined the polis; the pay is no that bad, and the work is naethin' tae an able-bodied man."

When these particulars had been digested by the audience -

"It's a crooded place London, and the fouks aye in a tiravie (commotion), rinnin' here an' rinnin' there, and the maist feck o' them dinna ken whar they're gaein.

"It's officer this and officer that frae mornin' till nicht. It's peetifu' tae see the helplessness o' the bodies in their ain toon. And they're freevolous," continued the figure, refreshing itself with a reminiscence.

"It wes this verra mornin' that a man askit me hoo tae get tae the Strand.

"'Haud on,' I says, 'till ye come tae a cross street, and dinna gang doon it, and when ye see anither pass it, but whup roond the third, and yir nose 'ill bring ye tae the Strand.'

"He was a shachlin bit cratur, and he lookit up at me.

"'Where were you born, officer?' in his clippit English tongue.

"'Drumtochty,' a' said, 'an' we hev juist ae man as sma' as you in the hale Glen.'

"He gied awa' lauchin' like tae split his sides, an' the fac' is there's no ane o' them asks me a question but he lauchs. They're a licht-headed fouk, and no sair educat. But we maunna boast; they hevna hed oor advantages."

The minister made a brave effort to assert himself.

"Is there anything I can do?" but the figure simply waved its hand and resumed:

"A'm comin' tae that, but a' thocht ye wud be wantin' ma opeenion o' London.

"Weel, ye see, the first thing a' did, of coorse, after settlin' doon, was tae gae roond the kirks and hear what kin' o' ministers they hae up here. A've been in saxteen kirks the last three months, an' a' wud hae been in mair had it no bin for ma oors.

"Ay, ay, a' ken ye 'ill be wantin' ma judgment," interpreting a movement in the chair, "an' ye 'ill hae it. Some wes puir stuff - plenty o' water and little meal - and some wesna sae bad for England. But ye 'ill be pleased to know," here the figure relaxed and beamed on the anxious minister, "that a'm rael weel satisfied wi' yersel', and a'm thinkin' o' sittin' under ye.

"Man," were Drumtochty's last words, "a' wish Elspeth Macfadyen cud hear ye, her 'at prees (tastes) the sermons in oor Glen; a' believe she wud pass ye, an' if ye got a certeeficat frae Elspeth, ye wud be a prood man."

Drumtochty read widely - Soutar was soaked in Carlyle, and Marget Howe knew her "In Memoriam" by heart - but our intellectual life centred on the weekly sermon. Men thought about Sabbath as they followed the plough in our caller air, and braced themselves for an effort at the giving out of the text. The hearer had his snuff and selected his attitude, and from that moment to the close he never moved nor took his eyes off the preacher. There was a tradition that one of the Disruption fathers had preached in the Free Kirk for one hour and fifty minutes on the bulwarks of Zion, and had left the impression that he was only playing round the outskirts of his subject. No preacher with anything to say could complain of Drumtochty, for he got a patient, honest, critical hearing from beginning to end. If a preacher were slightly equipped, the audience may have been trying. Well-meaning evangelists who came with what they called "a simple Gospel address," and were accustomed to have their warmer passages punctuated with rounds of spiritual applause in the shape of smiles and nods, lost heart in face of that judicial front, and afterwards described Drumtochty in the religious papers as "dead." It was as well that these good men walked in a vain show, for, as a matter of fact, their hearers were painfully alive.

"Whar did yon wakely body come frae, Burnbrae? it wes licht wark the day. There wes nae thocht worth mentionin', and onything he hed wes eked oot by repeetition. Tae sae naethin' o' bairnly stories."

"He lives aboot England, a'm telt, an' dis a feck o' gude in his ain place. He hesna muckle in his head, a'll alloo that, Netherton, but he's an earnest bit cratur."

"Ou ay, and fu' o' self-conceit. Did ye hear hoo often he said 'I'? a' got as far as saxty-three, and then a' lost coont. But a' keepit 'dear,' it cam tae the hundred neat.

"'Weel?' a' says tae Elspeth Macfadyen. A' kent she wud hae his measure.

"'Gruel, Netherton, juist gruel, and eneuch tae scunner (disgust) ye wi' sugar.'"

It was the birthright of every native of the parish to be a critic, and certain were allowed to be experts in special departments - Lachlan Campbell in doctrine and Jamie Soutar in logic - but as an old round practitioner Mrs. Macfadyen had a solitary reputation. It rested on a long series of unreversed judgments, with felicitous strokes of description that passed into the literary capital of the Glen. One felt it was genius, and could only note contributing circumstances - an eye that took in the preacher from the crown of his head to the sole of his foot; an almost uncannie insight into character; the instinct to seize on every scrap of evidence; a memory that was simply an automatic register; an unfailing sense of fitness; and an absolute impartiality regarding subject.

It goes without saying that Mrs. Macfadyen did not take nervous little notes during the sermon - all writing on Sabbath, in kirk or outside, was strictly forbidden in Drumtochty - or mark her Bible, or practise any other profane device of feeble-minded hearers. It did not matter how elaborate or how incoherent a sermon might be, it could not confuse our critic.

When John Peddie of Muirtown, who always approached two hours, and usually had to leave out the last head, took time at the Drumtochty Fast, and gave, at full length, his famous discourse on the total depravity of the human race, from the text, "Arise, shine, for thy light is come," it may be admitted that the Glen wavered in its confidence. Human nature has limitations, and failure would have been no discredit to Elspeth.

"They were sayin' at the Presbytery," Burnbrae reported, "that it hes mair than seeventy heads, coontin' pints, of coorse, and a' can weel believe it. Na, na, it's no tae be expeckit that Elspeth cud gie them a' aifter ae hearin'."

Jamie Souter looked in to set his mind at rest, and Elspeth went at once to work.

"Sit doon, Jamie, for it canna be dune in a meenut."

It took twenty-three minutes exactly, for Jamie watched the clock.

"That's the laist, makin' seeventy-four, and ye may depend on every ane but that fourth pint under the sixth head. Whether it wes the 'beginnin' o' faith' or 'the origin,' a' canna be sure, for he cleared his throat at the time."

Peter Bruce stood helpless at the Junction next Friday - Drumtochty was celebrating Elspeth - and the achievement established her for life.

Probationers who preached in the vacancy had heard rumours, and tried to identify their judge, with the disconcerting result that they addressed their floweriest passages to Mistress Stirton, who was the stupidest woman in the Free Kirk, and had once stuck in the "chief end of man." They never suspected the sonsy motherly woman, two pews behind Donald Menzies, with her face of demure interest and general air of country simplicity. It was as well for the probationers that they had not caught the glint of those black beady eyes.

"It's curious," Mrs. Macfadyen remarked to me one day, "hoo the pulpit fashions change, juist like weemen's bonnets.

"Noo a' mind when auld Doctor Ferintosh, him 'at wrote 'Judas Iscariot the first Residuary,' would stand twa meenutes facing the fouk, and no sit doon till he hed his snuff.

"But thae young birkies gie oot 'at they see naebody comin' in, an' cover their face wi' ae hand sae solemn, that if ye didna catch them keekin' through their fingers tae see what like the kirk is, ye wud think they were prayin'."

Beside the Bonnie Brier Bush   145

"There's not much escapes you," I dared to say, and although the excellent woman was not accessible to gross flattery, she seemed pleased.

"A'm thankfu' that a' can see withoot lookin'; an' a'll wager nae man ever read his sermon in Drumtochty Kirk, an' a' didna find him oot. Noo, there's the new minister o' Netheraird, he writes his sermon on ae side o' ten sheets o' paper, an' he's that carried awa' at the end o' ilka page that he disna ken what he's daein', an' the sleeve o' his goon slips the sheet across tae the ither side o' the Bible.

"But Doctor Ferintosh wes cleverer, sall it near beat me tae detect him," and Elspeth paused to enjoy the pulpit ruse. "It cam tae me sudden ae Sacrament Monday, hoo dis he aye turn up twal texts, naither mair nor less, and that set me thinkin'. Then a' noticed that he left the Bible open at the place till anither text was due, an' I wunnered a'd been sae slow. It wes this wy: he askit the beadle for a gless o' water in the vestry, and slippit his sermon in atween the leaves in sae mony bits. A've wished for a gallery at a time, but there's mair credit in findin' it oot below - ay, an' pleesure tae; a' never wearied in kirk in ma life."

Mrs. Macfadyen did not appreciate prodigal quotations of Scriptures, and had her suspicions of this practice.

"Tak the minister o' Pitscourie noo; he's fair fozzy wi' trokin' in his gairden an' feedin' pigs, and hesna studied a sermon for thirty year.

"Sae what dis he dae, think ye? He havers for a whilie on the errors o' the day, and syne he says, 'That's what man says, but what says the Apostle Paul? We shall see what the Apostle Paul says.' He puts on his glasses, and turns up the passage, and reads maybe ten verses, and then he's aff on the jundy (trot) again. When a man hes naethin' tae say he's aye lang, and a've seen him gie half an oor o' passages, and anither half oor o' havers.

"'He's a Bible preacher, at any rate,' says Burnbrae tae me laist Fast, for, honest man, he hes aye some gude word for a body.

"'It's ae thing,' I said to him, 'tae feed a calf wi' milk, and anither tae gie it the empty cogie tae lick.'

"It's curious, but a've noticed that when a Moderate gets lazy he preaches auld sermons, but a Free Kirk minister taks tae abusin' his neeburs and readin' screeds o' the Bible.

"But Maister Pittendreigh hes twa sermons, at ony rate," and Elspeth tasted the sweets of memory with such keen relish that I begged for a share.

"Well, ye see he's terrible prood o' his feenishes, and this is ane o' them:

"'Heaven, ma brethren, will be far grander than the hoose o' ony earthly potentate, for there ye will no longer eat the flesh of bulls nor drink the blood o' goats, but we shall sook the juicy pear and scoop the loocious meelon. Amen.'

"He hes nae mair sense o' humour than an owl, and a' aye haud that a man withoot humour sudna be allowed intae a poopit.

"A' hear that they have nae examination in humour at

the college; it's an awfu' want, for it wud keep oot mony a dreich body.

"But the meelon's naethin' tae the goat, that cowed a'thing, at the Fast tae.

"If Jeems wes aboot a' daurna mention 't: he canna behave himsel' tae this day gin he hears 'it, though ye ken he's a douce man as ever lived.

"It wes anither feenish, and it ran this wy:

"'Noo, ma freends, a' wull no be keepin' ye ony longer, and ye 'ill a' gae hame tae yir ain hooses and mind yir ain business. And as sune as ye get hame ilka man 'ill gae tae his closet and shut the door, and stand for five meenutes, and ask himsel' this solemn question, "Am I a goat?" Amen.'

"The amen near upset me masel', and a' hed tae dunge Jeems wi' ma elbow.

"He said no a word on the wy back, but a' saw it wes barmin' in him, and he gied oot sudden aifter his dinner as if he had been ta'en unweel.

"A' cam' on him in the byre, rowing in the strae like a bairn, and every ither row he took he wud say, 'Am I a goat?'

"It wes na cannie for a man o' his wecht, besides bein' a married man and a kirk member, and a' gied him a hearin'.

"He sobered doon, and a' never saw him dae the like since. But he hesna forgot, na, na; a've seen a look come ower Jeems' face in kirk, and a've been feared."

When the Free Kirk quarrelled in their vacancy over two probationers, Mrs. Macfadyen summed them up with such excellent judgment that they were thrown over and peace restored.

"There's some o' thae Muirtown drapers can busk oot their windows that ye canna pass withoot lookin'; there's bits o' blue and bits o' red, and a ribbon here an' a lace yonder.

"It's a bonnie show and denty, an' no wunner the lassies stan' and stare.

"But gae intae the shop, and peety me, there's next tae naethin'; it's a' in the window.

"Noo, that's Maister Popinjay, as neat an' fikey a little mannie as ever a' saw in a black goon.

"His bit sermon wes six poems - five a' hed heard afore - four anecdotes - three aboot himsel' and ain aboot a lord - twa burnies, ae floo'r gairden, and a snowstorm, wi' the text thirteen times and 'beloved' twal; that was a'; a takin' window, and Netherton's lassies cudna sleep thinkin' o' him.

"There's ither shopmen in Muirtown that fair scunner ye wi' their windows - they're that ill set out - and inside there's sic a wrale o' stuff that the man canna get what ye want; he's clean smoored wi' his ain goods.

"It's a graund shop for the auld fouk that hae plenty o' time and can turn ower the things by the 'oor. Ye 'ill no get a young body inside the door.

"That's Maister Auchtermuchty; he hes mair material than he kens hoo tae handle, and naebody, hearin' him, can mak head or tail o' his sermon.

"Ye get a rive at the Covenants ae meenute, and a mouthfu' o' justification the next. Yir nae suner wi' the Patriarchs than yir whuppit aff tae the Apostles.

"It's rich feedin', nae doot, but sair mixed, an' no verra tasty."

So the old and young compromised, and chose Carmichael.

Elspeth was candid enough on occasion, but she was not indiscreet. She could convey her mind delicately if need be, and was a mistress of subtle suggestion.

When Netherton's nephew preached the missionary sermon - he was a stout young man with a volcanic voice - Mrs. Macfadyen could not shirk her duty, but she gave her judgment with care.

"He's a fine lad, and 'ill be sure to get a kirk; he's been weel brocht up, and comes o' decent fouk.

"His doctrine soonds richt, and he 'ill no gang aff the track. Ye canna ca' him bashfu', and he's sure to be heard."

Her audience still waited, and not in vain.

"But the Lord hes nae pleesure in the legs o' a man," and every one felt that the last word had been said on Netherton's nephew.

Ian Maclaren

II

THE COLLAPSE OF MRS. MACFADYEN

Carmichael used to lament bitterly that he had lost his
Gaelic, and laboured plans of compensation for our
Celts, who were understood to worship in English at an
immense reduction of profit. One spring he intercepted
a Highland minister, who was returning from his
winter's raid on Glasgow with great spoil, and arranged
an evening service, which might carry Lachlan
Campbell back to the golden days of Auchindarroch.
Mr. Dugald Mactavish was himself much impressed
with the opportunity of refreshing his exiled brethren,
speaking freely on the Saturday of the Lowlands as
Babylon, and the duty of gathering the outcasts of
Israel into one. He was weaned with difficulty from
Gaelic, and only consented to preach in the "other
language" on condition that he should not be restricted
in time. His soul had been much hampered in West
End churches, where he had to appeal for his new
stove under the first head, lest he should go empty
away, and it was natural for one escaping from such
bondage to put a generous interpretation on
Carmichael's concession. So Maister Dugald continued
unto the setting of the sun. His discourse was so rich
and varied that Peddie of Muirtown on original sin was
not to be compared with it in breadth of treatment, and
Mrs. Macfadyen confessed frankly that she gave up in

despair before the preacher had fairly entered on his second hour. Besides the encounter of the preacher with Mr. Urijah Hopps, which carried the Glen by storm, and kept the name of Mactavish green with us for a generation.

Rumours of this monumental pulpit effort, with its stirring circumstances, passed from end to end of the Glen during the week, and Peter himself recognised that it was an occasion at the Junction on Friday.

"Ye may as weel shut aff the steam, Jeems," Peter explained to our engine-driver, "an' gie them ten meenuts. It's been by ordinar' at Drumtochty Free Kirk laist Sabbath nicht, and Drumsheugh 'ill no move till he hears the end o't."

And as soon as the Muirtown train had removed all strangers, that worthy man opened the campaign.

"What kin' o' collieshangie (disturbance) is this ye've been carryin' on, Hillocks? it's doonricht aggravatin' that ye're no content pesterin' oor life oot wi' that English body in the kirkyaird, but ye maist needs set him up tae arglebargle wi' a stranger minister at the Free Kirk. They say that the puir man cud hardly get a word in atween you and yir lodger. Burnbrae here is threatenin' ye wi' the Sherra, and a' dinna wonder.

"It's nae lauchin' maitter, a' can tell ye, Drumsheugh; a've never been sae black affrontit a' ma life. Burnbrae kens as weel as ye dae that a' wasna tae blame.

"Ye 'ill better clear yersel at ony rate, Hillocks, for some o' the neeburs threep (insist) 'at it wes you, and some that it wes yir freend, an' there's ithers declare ye ran in compt (company) like twa dogs worrying sheep; it wes a bonnie like pliskie (escapade) onywy, and hardly fit for an Auld Kirk elder" - a sally much enjoyed by the audience, who knew that, after Whinnie, Hillocks was the doucest man in Drumtochty.

"Weel, ye see it wes this wy," began Hillocks, with the air of a man on his trial for fire raising. "Hopps fund oot that a Hielandman wes tae preach in the Free Kirk, and naethin' wud sateesfy him but that we maun gae. A' micht hae jaloused (suspected) it wesna the sermon the wratch wantit, for he hed the impidence tae complain that the Doctor was tedious Sabbath a fort-nicht when he gied us 'Ruth,' though I never minded 'Ruth' gae aff sae sweet a' the times a've heard it.

"Gin a' hed imagined what the ettercap (captious creature) wes aifter a' wud hae seen ma feet in the fire afore they carried me tae the Free Kirk that nicht.

"Says he tae me on the road, 'A'm told the minister will be in his national costume.'

"'He 'ill be in his goon and bands,' says I, 'if that's what ye mean,' for the head o' him is fu' o' maggots, and nae man can tell what he wull be at next.

"'Mister Soutar said that he would wear his kilt, and that it would be an interesting spectacle.'

"'Jamie's been drawing yir leg (befooling you),' says I. 'Man, there's naebody wears a kilt forbye gemkeepers and tourist bodies. Ye 'ill better come awa hame,' and sall, if a' hed kent what wes tae happen, a' wud hae taken him aff below ma oxter.

"It's no richt tae mak me responsible, for a' tried tae wile him awa tae the back o' the kirk whar naebody cud see him, but he's that thrawn and upsettin', if he didna gae tae the verra front seat afore the poopit.

"'I want a good position,' says he; 'I'll see everything here;' sae a' left him an' gied tae Elspeth Macfadyen's seat.

"'He's anxious tae hear,' she said, 'an' a'm thinkin' he 'ill get mair than he expecks. A' wish it wes weel ower masel, Hillocks; it 'ill be an awfu' nicht.'

"Thae Hielandmen dinna pit aff time wi' the preleeminaries, but they were lang eneuch tae let onybody see what kin' o' man Mactavish wes.

"A gruesome carle, neeburs, wi' his hair hangin' roond his face like a warlock and his een blazin' oot o' his head like fire; the sicht o' him is sure tae sober Hopps, thinks I.

"But no, there's some fouk 'ill tak nae warnin'; there he was, sittin' in front o' Mactavish with his thumbs in his airm holes, and a watch gaird spread richt across him, and ae leg cocked over the ither, the verra eemage of a bantam cock fleein' in the face o' judgment."

Drumtochty had never moved during this history, and now they drew closer round Hillocks, on whom the mantle of speech had for once descended.

"Mactavish lookit at the body aince, and he lookit again juist tae gie him fair notis, and then he broke oot in face o' the hale congregation:

"'There's nothing in all the world so deceptive as sin, for outside it's like a bonnie summer day, and inside it's as black as hell.

"'Now here iss this fat little man sittin' before me with his suit o' blue clothes so bonnie and dainty, and a watch guard as thick as my finger on his wame, smilin' an' smirkin', and real well contented with himself, but if he wass opened up what a sight it would be for men and angels. Oh yes, yes, it would be a fearsome sicht, and no man here would be able to look.'

"A' tell ye, neeburs, ye micht hae heard a pin fa' tae the ground, and ma heart was thumping in ma briest; a' wudna come thro' the like o' yon again for half the pleenishin' o' Hillocks."

There was not a sound at the junction save the steam escaping from the engine, and Hillocks resumed:

"But the worst's comin'. Hopps jumps up and faces Mactavish - a'll no deny there is some spunk in the body.

"'What right have you to speak like that to me? do you know who I am?'

"He hed better been quiet, for he wes nae match for yon Hielandman.

"Mactavish glowered at him for maybe a meenut till the puir cratur fell back intae his seat.

"'Man,' says Mactavish, 'I do not know who you are, and I do not know what you are, and I shall not be asking who you are, and I am not caring though you be

MacCallummore himsel'. You are just a Parable, oh yes, just a Parable.

"'But if ye be convicted of secret sin ye may go out, and if there be anybody else whose sins have been laid bare he may go out too, and if nobody wants to go out, then I will be going on with the sermon, oh yes, for it will not do to be spending all our time on Parables.'

"As sure as a'm stannin' here ye cudna see Hopps inside his claithes when Mactavish wes dune wi' him."

When the train started Hillocks received the compliments of the third with much modesty, and added piquant details regarding the utter confusion of our sermon taster.

"'Did ye follow?' a' speirit o' Elspeth afore a' went tae pit Hopps thegither.

"'Cud a' follow a bumbee?' was the only word a' got frae her; a' saw she was beaten for aince and wes rael mad."

"I'st true Elspeth scuffled wi' her feet at the laist head and gar'd him close?"

"A'll neither deny nor affirm, Drumsheugh; but there's nae doot when the mune began tae shine aboot nine, and Mactavish started aff on the Devil, somebody scrapit aside me. It wesna Jeems; he daurna for his life; and it wesna me. A'll no say but it micht be Elspeth, but she wes sair provokit. Aifter haddin' her ain twenty years tae be maistered by a Hielandman."

It was simply a duty of friendship to look in and

Ian Maclaren

express one's sympathy with Mrs. Macfadyen in this professional disaster. I found her quite willing to go over the circumstances, which were unexampled in her experience, and may indeed be considered a contribution to history.

"A' wudna hae minded," explained Elspeth, settling down to narrative, "hoo mony heads he gied oot, no tho' he hed titched the hundred. A've cause tae be gratefu' for a guid memory, and a've kept it in fine fettle wi' sermons. My wy is tae place ilka head at the end o' a shelf and a' the pints aifter it in order like the plates there," and Mrs. Macfadyen pointed with honest pride to her wall of crockery, "and when the minister is at an illustration or makin' an appeal a' aye rin ower the rack tae see that a've a' the pints in their places. Maister Mactavish cud ne'er hae got the wheephand o' me wi' his diveesions; he's no fit to haud the can'le tae John Peddie. Na, na, a' wesna feared o' that when a' examined yon man gieing oot the Psalm, but a' didna like his een.

"'He's ravelled,' a' said tae masel, 'without beginning or end; we 'ill hae a nicht o't,' and sae we hed."

I preserved a sympathetic silence till Mrs. Macfadyen felt herself able to proceed.

"It's easy eneuch, ye see, for an auld hand tae manage ae set o' heads gin they come tae ten or a hundred, but it's another business when a man hes different sets in ae sermon. Noo hoo mony sets div ye think that man hed afore he wes dune?"

It was vain for a mere layman to cope with the possibilities of Mr. Mactavish.

"Fower, as a'm a leevin' woman, and that's no a'; he didna feenish wi' ae set an' begin wi' the next, but if he didna mix them a' thegither. Fower set o' heads a' in a tangle; noo ye hae some kin' o' idea o' what a' hed tae face." And Mrs. Macfadyen paused that I might take in the situation.

When I expressed my conviction that even the most experienced hearer was helpless in such circumstances, Elspeth rallied, and gave me to understand that she had saved some fragments from the wreckage.

"A'll juist tell ye the hale hypothic, for sic a discoorse ye may never hear a' the days o' yir life.

"Ye ken thae Hielandmen tak their texts for the maist pairt frae the Auld Testament, and this was it mair or less, 'The trumpet shall be blown, and they shall come from Assyria and the land o' Egypt,' and he began by explainin' that there were twa classes in Drumtochty, those who were born and bred in the parish, which were oursels, and them 'at hed tae stay here owin' tae the mysterious dispensations o' Providence, which wes Lachlan Campbell.

"Noo this roosed ma suspicions, for it's against reason for a man tae be dividing intae classes till the end o' his sermon. Tak my word, it's no chancy when a minister begins at the tail o' his subject: he'll wind a queer pirn afore he's dune.

"Weel, he gaed up and he gaed doon, and he aye said, 'Oh yes, yes,' juist like the thrashing mill at Drumsheugh scraiking and girling till it's fairly aff, an' by-and-by oot he comes wi' his heads.

"'There are fower trumpets,' says he. 'First, a leeteral trumpet; second, a heestorical trumpet; third, a metaphorical trumpet; fourth, a speeritual trumpet.'

"'I've got ye,' a' said tae masel, and settled doon to hear him on the first head, for fear he micht hae pints; but wull ye believe me, he barely mentioned leeteral till he was aff tae speeritual, and then back tae heestorical, an' in five meenuts he had the hale fower trumpets blawing thegither.

"It wes maist exasperatin', and a' saw Jeems watchin' me - but that's naethin'.

"'There be many trumpets,' says he, 'oh yes, an' it wes a good trumpet Zaccheus heard,' and afore a' knew where a' wes he hed startit again wi' fower new heads, as if he had never said trumpet.

"'A big tree' he cries, 'an' a little man, oh yes, an' this is what we will be doin'.

"'First. We shall go up the tree wi' Zaccheus.

"'Second. We shall sit in the branches wi' Zaccheus.

"'Third. We shall come down from the tree wi' Zaccheus; and if time permits,

"'Fourth. We shall be going home wi' the publican.'"

It seemed only just to pay a tribute at this point to the wonderful presence of mind Mrs. Macfadyen had shown amid unparalleled difficulties.

"Hoot awa," she responded; the meenut ony heads cam

a' knew ma grund: but the times atween I wes fairly lost.

"A'll no deny," and our critic turned aside to general reflections, "that Mactavish said mony bonnie and affeckin' things frae time tae time, like the glimpses o' the hills ye get when the mist rolls awa, and he cam nearer the hert than the feck o' oor preachers; but certes yon confusion is mair than us low country fouk cud stand.

"Juist when he wes speakin' aboot Zaccheus as nice as ye please - though whether he was up the tree or doon the tree a' cudna for the life o' me tell - he stops sudden and looks at us ower the top o' his spectacles, which is terrible impressive, and near dis instead o' speakin.'

"We will now come to the third head of this discoorse.

"'The trumpet shall be blown, for,' says he, in a kin' o' whisper, 'there's a hint o' oppeesition here,' an' a' tell ye honestly a' lost hert a'thegither, for here he wes back again amang the trumpets, and a'll gie ma aith he never sae much as mentioned that head afore.

"It's an awfu' peety that some men dinna ken when tae stop; they micht see frae the poopit; if a' saw the tears comin' tae the women's een, or the men glowering like wild cats for fear they sud brak doon, a'd say Amen as quick as Pittendreigh aifter his goat.

"What possessed Maister Dugald, as Lachlan ca'd him, a'd dinna ken, but aboot half nine - an' he begood at six - he sat oot upon the trumpets again, an' when he cudna get a haud o' them, he says:

"'It will be getting dark' (the mune was fairly oot), 'an' it is time we were considering our last head.

"'We will now study Satan in all his offices and characteristics.'"

"A' see they've been telling ye what happened," and confusion covered Mrs. Macfadyen's ingenuous countenance.

"Weel, as sure's deith a' cudna help it, tae be sittin' on peens for mair than twa oors tryin' tae get a grup o' a man's heads, an' him tae play hide-and-seek wi' ye, an' then tae begin on Satan at nine o'clock is mair nor flesh and bluid cud endure.

"A' acknowledge a' scrapit, but a' houp tae gudeness a'll never be tempted like yon again.

"It's a judgment on me for ma pride, an' Jeems said that tae me, for a' boastit a' cudna be beat, but anither oor o' Mactavish wud hae driven me dottle (silly)."

Then I understood that Mrs. Macfadyen had been humbled in the dust.

A DOCTOR OF THE OLD SCHOOL

I

A GENERAL PRACTITIONER

Drumtochty was accustomed to break every law of health, except wholesome food and fresh air, and yet had reduced the Psalmist's farthest limit to an average life-rate. Our men made no difference in their clothes for summer or winter, Drumsheugh and one or two of the larger farmers condescending to a topcoat on Sabbath, as a penalty of their position, and without regard to temperature. They wore their blacks at a funeral, refusing to cover them with anything, out of respect to the deceased, and standing longest in the kirkyard when the north wind was blowing across a hundred miles of snow. If the rain was pouring at the Junction, then Drumtochty stood two minutes longer through sheer native dourness till each man had a cascade from the tail of his coat, and hazarded the suggestion, halfway to Kildrummie, that it had been "a bit scrowie," a "scrowie" being as far short of a "shoor" as a "shoor" fell below "weet."

This sustained defiance of the elements provoked occasional judgments in the shape of a "hoast" (cough), and the head of the house was then exhorted by his women folk to "change his feet" if he had

Ian Maclaren

happened to walk through a burn on his way home, and was pestered generally with sanitary precautions. It is right to add that the gudeman treated such advice with contempt, regarding it as suitable for the effeminacy of towns, but not seriously intended for Drumtochty. Sandy Stewart "napped" stones on the road in his shirt sleeves, wet or fair, summer and winter, till he was persuaded to retire from active duty at eighty-five, and he spent ten years more in regetting his hastiness and criticising his successor. The ordinary course of life, with fine air and contented minds, was to do a full share of work till seventy, and then to look after "orra" jobs well into the eighties, and to "slip awa" within sight of ninety. Persons above ninety were understood to be acquitting themselves with credit, and assumed airs of authority, brushing aside the opinions of seventy as immature, and confirming their conclusions with illustrations drawn from the end of last century.

When Hillocks' brother so far forgot himself as to "slip awa" at sixty, that worthy man was scandalized, and offered laboured explanations at the "beerial."

"It's an awfu' business ony wy ye look at it, an' a sair trial tae us a'. A' never heard tell o' sic a thing in oor family afore, an' it's no easy accoontin' for't.

"The gudewife was sayin' he wes never the same sin' a weet nicht he lost himsel on the muir and slept below a bush; but that's neither here nor there. A'm thinkin' he sappit his constitution thae twa years he wes grieve aboot England. That wes thirty years syne, but ye're never the same aifter thae foreign climates."

Drumtochty listened patiently to Hillocks' apologia, but was not satisfied.

"It's clean havers aboot the muir. Losh keep's, we've a' sleepit oot and never been a hair the waur.

"A' admit that England micht hae dune the job; it's no cannie stravagin' yon wy frae place tae place, but Drums never complained tae me as if he hed been nippit in the Sooth."

The parish had, in fact, lost confidence in Drums after his wayward experiment with a potato-digging machine, which turned out a lamentable failure, and his premature departure confirmed our vague impression of his character.

"He's awa noo," Drumsheugh summed up, after opinion had time to form; "an' there were waur fouk than Drums, but there's nae doot he wes a wee flichty."

When illness had the audacity to attack a Drumtochty man, it was described as a "whup," and was treated by the men with a fine negligence. Hillocks was sitting in the Post Office one afternoon when I looked in for my letters, and the right side of his face was blazing red. His subject of discourse was the prospects of the turnip "breer," but he casually explained that he was waiting for medical advice.

"The gudewife is keepin' up a ding-dong frae mornin' till nicht aboot ma face, and a'm fair deaved (deafened), so a'm watchin' for MacLure tae get a bottle as he comes wast; yon's him noo."

The doctor made his diagnosis from horseback on sight, and stated the result with that admirable clearness which endeared him to Drumtochty.

"Confoond ye, Hillocks, what are ye ploiterin' aboot here for in the weet wi' a face like a boiled beet? Div ye no ken that ye've a titch o' the rose (erysipelas), and ocht tae be in the hoose? Gae hame wi' ye afore a' leave the bit, and send a haflin for some medicine. Ye donnerd idiot, are ye ettlin tae follow Drums afore yir time?" And the medical attendant of Drumtochty continued his invective till Hillocks started, and still pursued his retreating figure with medical directions of a simple and practical character.

"A'm watchin', an' peety ye if ye pit aff time. Keep yir bed the mornin', and dinna show yir face in the fields till a' see ye. A'll gie ye a cry on Monday - sic an auld fule - but there's no ane o' them tae mind anither in the hale pairish."

Hillocks' wife informed the kirkyaird that the doctor "gied the gudeman an awfu' clearin'," and that Hillocks "wes keepin' the hoose," which meant that the patient had tea breakfast, and at that time was wandering about the farm buildings in an easy undress with his head in a plaid.

It was impossible for a doctor to earn even the most modest competence from a people of such scandalous health, and so MacLure had annexed neighbouring parishes. His house - little more than a cottage - stood on the roadside among the pines towards the head of our Glen, and from this base of operations he dominated the wild glen that broke the wall of the Grampians above Drumtochty - where the snows drifts were twelve feet deep in winter, and the only way of passage at times was the channel of the river - and the moorland district westwards till he came to the Dunleith sphere of influence, where there were four doctors and a hydropathic. Drumtochty in its length, which was eight miles, and its breadth, which was four, lay in his hand; besides a glen behind, unknown to the world, which in the night time he visited at the risk of life, for the way thereto was across the big moor with its peat holes and treacherous bogs. And he held the land eastwards towards Muirtown so far as Geordie, the Drumtochty post, travelled every day, and could carry word that the doctor was wanted. He did his best for the need of every man, woman, and child in this wild, straggling district, year in, year out, in the snow and in the heat, in the dark and in the light, without rest, and without holiday for forty years.

One horse could not do the work of this man, but we liked best to see him on his old white mare, who died the week after her master, and the passing of the two did our hearts good. It was not that he rode beautifully, for he broke every canon of art, flying with his arms, stooping till he seemed to be speaking into Jess's ears, and rising in the saddle beyond all necessity. But he could rise faster, stay longer in the saddle, and had a firmer grip with his knees than any one I ever met, and it was all for mercy's sake. When the reapers in harvest time saw a figure whirling past in a cloud of dust, or the family at the foot of Glen Urtach, gathered round the fire on a winter's night, heard the rattle of a horse's hoofs on the road, or the shepherds, out after the sheep, traced a black speck moving across the snow to the upper glen, they knew it was the doctor, and, without being conscious of it, wished him God speed.

Before and behind his saddle were strapped the instruments and medicines the doctor might want, for he never knew what was before him. There were no specialists in Drumtochty, so this man had to do everything as best he could, and as quickly. He was chest doctor and doctor for every other organ as well; he was accoucheur and surgeon; he was oculist and aurist; he was dentist and chloroformist, besides being chemist and druggist. It was often told how he was far up Glen Urtach when the feeders of the threshing mill caught young Burnbrae, and how he only stopped to change horses at his house, and galloped all the way to Burnbrae, and flung himself off his horse and amputated the arm, and saved the lad's life.

"You wud hae thocht that every meenut was an hour," said Jamie Soutar, who had been at the threshing, "an' a'll never forget the puir lad lying as white as deith on the floor o' the loft, wi' his head on a sheaf, an' Burnbrae haudin' the bandage ticht an' prayin' a' the while, and the mither greetin' in the corner.

"'Will he never come?' she cries, an' a' heard the soond o' the horse's feet on the road a mile awa in the frosty air.

"'The Lord be praised!' said Burnbrae, and a' slippit doon the ladder as the doctor came skelpin' intae the close, the foam fleein' frae his horse's mooth.

"'Whar is he?' wes a' that passed his lips, an' in five meenuts he hed him on the feedin' board, and wes at his wark - sic wark, neeburs - but he did it weel. An' ae thing a' thocht rael thochtfu' o' him: he first sent aff the laddie's mither tae get a bed ready.

"'Noo that's feenished, and his constitution 'ill dae the rest,' and he carried the lad doon the ladder in his airms like a bairn, and laid him in his bed, and waits aside him till he wes sleepin', and then says he: 'Burnbrae, yir a gey lad never tae say "Collie, will ye lick?" for a' hevna tasted meat for saxteen hoors.'

"It was michty tae see him come intae the yaird that day, neeburs; the verra look o' him wes victory."

Jamie's cynicism slipped off in the enthusiasm of this reminiscence, and he expressed the feeling of Drumtochty. No one sent for MacLure save in great straits, and the sight of him put courage in sinking hearts. But this was not by the grace of his appearance, or the advantage of a good bedside manner. A tall, gaunt, loosely made man, without an ounce of superfluous flesh on his body, his face burned a dark brick colour by constant exposure to the weather, red hair and beard turning grey, honest blue eyes that look you ever in the face, huge hands with wrist bones like the shank of a ham, and a voice that hurled his salutations across two fields, he suggested the moor rather than the drawing-room. But what a clever hand it was in an operation, as delicate as a woman's, and what a kindly voice it was in the humble room where the shepherd's wife was weeping by her man's bedside. He was "ill pitten thegither" to begin with, but many of his physical defects were the penalties of his work, and endeared him to the Glen. That ugly scar that cut into his right eyebrow and gave him such a sinister expression, was got one night Jess slipped on the ice and laid him insensible eight miles from home. His limp marked the big snowstorm in the fifties, when his horse missed the road in Glen Urtach, and they rolled together in a drift. MacLure escaped with a broken leg and the fracture of three ribs, but he never walked like other men again. He could not swing himself into the saddle without making two attempts and holding Jess's mane. Neither can you "warstle" through the peat bogs

Ian Maclaren

and snow drifts for forty winters without a touch of rheumatism. But they were honourable scars, and for such risks of life men get the Victoria Cross in other fields. MacLure got nothing but the secret affection of the Glen, which knew that none had ever done one-tenth as much for it as this ungainly, twisted, battered figure, and I have seen a Drumtochty face soften at the sight of MacLure limping to his horse.

Mr. Hopps earned the ill-will of the Glen for ever by criticising the doctor's dress, but indeed it would have filled any townsman with amazement. Black he wore once a year, on Sacrament Sunday, and, if possible, at a funeral; topcoat or waterproof never. His jacket and waistcoat were rough homespun of Glen Urtach wool, which threw off the wet like a duck's back, and below he was clad in shepherd's tartan trousers, which disappeared into unpolished riding boots. His shirt was grey flannel, and he was uncertain about a collar, but certain as to a tie which he never had, his beard doing instead, and his hat was soft felt of four colours and seven different shapes. His point of distinction in dress was the trousers, and they were the subject of unending speculation.

"Some threep that he's worn thae eedentical pair the last twenty year, an' a' mind masel him gettin' a tear ahint, when he was crossin' oor palin', and the mend's still veesible.

"Ithers declare 'at he's got a wab o' claith, and hes a new pair made in Muirtown aince in the twa year maybe, and keeps them in the garden till the new look wears aft.

"For ma ain pairt , " Soutar used to declare, "a' canna

mak up my mind, but there's ae thing sure, the Glen wud not like tae see him withoot them: it wud be a shock tae confidence. There's no muckle o' the check left, but ye can aye tell it, and when ye see thae breeks comin' in ye ken that if human pooer can save yir bairn's life it 'ill be dune."

The confidence of the Glen - and tributary states - was unbounded, and rested partly on long experience of the doctor's resources, and partly on his hereditary connection.

"His father was here afore him," Mrs. Macfadyen used to explain; "atween them they've hed the countyside for weel on tae a century; if MacLure disna understand oor constitution, wha dis, a' wud like tae ask?"

For Drumtochty had its own constitution and a special throat disease, as became a parish which was quite self-contained between the woods and the hills, and not dependent on the lowlands either for its diseases or its doctors.

"He's a skilly man, Doctor MacLure," continued my friend Mrs. Macfadyen, whose judgment on sermons or anything else was seldom at fault; "an' a kind-hearted, though o' coorse he hes his faults like us a', an' he disna tribble the Kirk often.

"He aye can tell what's wrang wi' a body, an' maistly he can put ye richt, and there's nae new-fangled wys wi' him: a blister for the ootside an' Epsom salts for the inside dis his wark, an' they say there's no an herb on the hills he disna ken.

" If we're tae dee, we're tae dee; an' if we're tae live,

we're tae live," concluded Elspeth, with sound Calvinistic logic; "but a'll say this for the doctor, that whether yir tae live or dee, he can aye keep up a shairp meisture on the skin.

"But he's no verra ceevil gin ye bring him when there's naethin' wrang," and Mrs. Macfadyen's face reflected another of Mr. Hopps' misadventures of which Hillocks held the copyright.

"Hopps' laddie ate grosarts (gooseberries) till they hed to sit up a' nicht wi' him, an' naethin' wud do but they maun hae the doctor, an' he writes 'immediately' on a slip o' paper.

"Weel, MacLure had been awa a' nicht wi' a shepherd's wife Dunleith wy, and he comes here withoot drawin' bridle, mud up tae the een.

"'What's a dae here, Hillocks?" he cries; 'it's no an accident, is't?' and when he got aff his horse he cud hardly stand wi' stiffness and tire.

"'It's nane o' us, doctor; it's Hopps' laddie; he's been eatin' ower mony berries.'

"If he didna turn on me like a tiger.

"'Div ye mean tae say - '

"'Weesht, weesht,' an' I tried tae quiet him, for Hopps wes comin' oot.

"'Well, doctor,' begins he, as brisk as a magpie, 'you're here at last; there's no hurry with you Scotchmen. My boy has been sick all night, and I've never had one wink of sleep. You might have come a little quicker, that's all I've got to say.'

"'We've mair tae dae in Drumtochty than attend tae every bairn that hes a sair stomach,' and a' saw MacLure wes roosed.

"'I'm astonished to hear you speak. Our doctor at home always says to Mrs. 'Opps, "Look on me as a family friend, Mrs. 'Opps, and send for me though it be only a headache."'

"'He'd be mair sparin' o' his offers if he hed four and twenty mile tae look aifter. There's naethin' wrang wi' yir laddie but greed. Gie him a gude dose o' castor oil and stop his meat for a day, an' he 'ill be a' richt the morn.'

"'He 'ill not take castor oil, doctor. We have given up those barbarous medicines.'

"'Whatna kind o' medicines hae ye noo in the Sooth?'

"'Well, you see, Dr. MacLure, we're homoeopathists, and I've my little chest here, 'and oot Hopps comes wi' his boxy.

"'Let's see't,' an' MacLure sits doon and taks oot the bit bottles, and he reads the names wi' a lauch every time.

"'Belladonna; did ye ever hear the like? Aconite; it cowes a'. Nux Vomica. What next? Weel, ma mannie,' he says tae Hopps, 'it's a fine ploy, and ye 'ill better gang on wi' the Nux till it's dune, and gie him ony ither o' the sweeties he fancies.

Ian Maclaren

"'Noo, Hillocks, a' maun be aff tae see Drumsheugh's grieve, for he's doon wi' the fever, and it's tae be a teuch fecht. A' hinna time tae wait for dinner; gie me some cheese an' cake in ma haund, and Jess 'ill tak a pail o' meal an' water.

"'Fee; a'm no wantin' yir fees, man; wi' that boxy ye dinna need a doctor; na, na, gie yir siller tae some puir body, Maister Hopps,' an' he was doon the road as hard as he cud lick."

His fees were pretty much what the folk chose to give him, and he collected them once a year at Kildrummie fair.

"Weel, doctor, what am a' awin' ye for the wife and bairn? Ye 'ill need three notes for that nicht ye stayed in the hoose an' a' the veesits."

"Havers," MacLure would answer, "prices are low, a'm hearing; gie's thirty shillings."

"No, a'll no, or the wife 'ill tak ma ears off," and it was settled for two pounds.

Lord Kilspindie gave him a free house and fields, and one way or other, Drumsheugh told me, the doctor might get in about £150 a year, out of which he had to pay his old housekeeper's wages and a boy's, and keep two horses, besides the cost of instruments and books, which he bought through a friend in Edinburgh with much judgment.

There was only one man who ever complained of the doctor's charges, and that was the new farmer of Milton, who was so good that he was above both churches, and held a meeting in his barn. (It was Milton the Glen supposed at first to be a Mormon, but I can't go into that now.) He offered McLure a pound less than he asked, and two tracts, whereupon MacLure expressed his opinion of Milton, both from a theological and social standpoint, with such vigour and frankness that an attentive audience of Drumtochty men could hardly contain themselves.

Jamie Soutar was selling his pig at the time, and missed the meeting, but he hastened to condole with Milton, who was complaining everywhere of the doctor's language.

"Ye did richt tae resist him; it 'ill maybe roose the Glen tae mak a stand; he fair hauds them in bondage.

"Thirty shillings for twal veesits, and him no mair than seeven mile awa, an' a'm telt there werena mair than four at nicht.

"Ye 'ill hae the sympathy o' the Glen, for a' body kens yir as free wi' yir siller as yir tracts.

"Wes't 'Beware o' gude warks' ye offered him? Man, ye chose it weel, for he's been colleckin' sae mony thae forty years, a'm feared for him.

"A've often thocht oor doctor's little better than the Gude Samaritan, an' the Pharisees didna think muckle o' his chance aither in this warld or that which is tae come."

II

THROUGH THE FLOOD

Doctor MacLure did not lead a solemn procession from the sick bed to the dining-room, and give his opinion from the hearthrug with an air of wisdom bordering on the supernatural, because neither the Drumtochty houses nor his manners were on that large scale. He was accustomed to deliver himself in the yard, and to conclude his directions with one foot in the stirrup; but when he left the room where the life of Annie Mitchell was ebbing slowly away, our doctor said not one word, and at the sight of his face her husband's heart was troubled.

He was a dull man, Tammas, who could not read the meaning of a sign, and laboured under a perpetual disability of speech; but love was eyes to him that day, and a mouth.

"Is't as bad as yir lookin', doctor? tell's the truth; wull Annie no come through?" and Tammas looked MacLure straight in the face, who never flinched his duty or said smooth things.

"A' wud gie onything tae say Annie hes a chance, but a' daurna; a' doot yir gaein' tae lose her, Tammas."

MacLure was in the saddle, and as he gave his judgment, he laid his hand on Tammas's shoulder with one of the rare caresses that pass between men.

"It's a sair business, but ye 'ill play the man and no vex Annie; she 'ill dae her best, a'll warrant."

"An' a'll dae mine," and Tammas gave MacLure's hand a grip that would have crushed the bones of a weakling. Drumtochty felt in such moments the brotherliness of this rough-looking man, and loved him.

Tammas hid his face in Jess's mane, who looked round with sorrow in her beautiful eyes, for she had seen many tragedies, and in this silent sympathy the stricken man drank his cup, drop by drop.

"A' wesna prepared for this, for a' aye thocht she wud live the langest.... She's younger than me by ten years, and never wes ill.... We've been mairit twal year laist Martinmas, but its juist like a year the day.... A' wes never worthy o' her, the bonniest, snoddest (neatest), kindliest lass in the Glen.... A' never cud mak oot hoo she ever lookit at me, 'at hesna hed ae word tae say aboot her till it's ower late.... She didna cuist up tae me that a' wesna worthy o' her, no her, but aye she said, 'Yir ma ain gudeman, and nane cud be kinder tae me.'... An' a' wes minded tae be kind, but a' see noo mony little trokes a' micht hae dune for her, and noo the time is bye.... Naebody kens hoo patient she wes wi' me, and aye made the best o' me, an' never pit me tae shame afore the fouk.... An' we never hed ae cross word, no ane in twal year.... We were mair nor man and wife, we were sweethearts a' the time.... Oh, ma bonnie lass, what 'ill the bairnies an' me dae withoot ye, Annie?"

The winter night was falling fast, the snow lay deep upon the ground, and the merciless north wind moaned through the close as Tammas wrestled with his sorrow dry-eyed, for tears were denied Drumtochty men. Neither the doctor nor Jess moved hand or foot, but their hearts were with their fellow creature, and at length the doctor made a sign to Marget Howe, who had come out in search of Tammas, and now stood by his side.

"Dinna mourn tae the brakin' o' yir hert, Tammas," she said, "as if Annie an' you hed never luved. Neither death nor time can pairt them that luve; there's naethin' in a' the warld sae strong as luve. If Annie gaes frae the sicht o' yir een she 'ill come the nearer tae yir hert. She wants tae see ye, and tae hear ye say that ye 'ill never forget her nicht nor day till ye meet in the land where there's nae pairtin'. Oh, a' ken what a'm sayin', for it's five year noo sin George gied awa, an' he's mair wi' me noo than when he wes in Edinboro' and I wes in Drumtochty."

"Thank ye kindly, Marget; thae are gude words and true, an' ye hev the richt tae say them; but a' canna dae without seein' Annie comin' tae meet me in the gloamin', an' gaein' in an' oot the hoose, an' hearin' her ca' me by ma name, an' a'll no can tell her that a' luve her when there's nae Annie in the hoose.

"Can naethin' be dune, doctor? Ye savit Flora Cammil, and young Burnbrae, an' yon shepherd's wife Dunleith wy, an' we were a sae prood o' ye, an' pleased tae think that ye hed keepit deith frae anither hame. Can ye no think o' somethin' tae help Annie, and gie her back tae her man and bairnies?" and Tammas searched the doctor's face in the cold, weird light.

"There's nae pooer in heaven or airth like luve," Marget said to me afterwards; "it maks the weak strong and the dumb tae speak. Oor herts were as water afore Tammas's words, an' a' saw the doctor shake in his saddle. A' never kent till that meenut hoo he hed a share in a'body's grief, an' carried the heaviest wecht o' a' the Glen. A' peetied him wi' Tammas lookin' at him sae wistfully, as if he hed the keys o' life an' deith in his hands. But he wes honest, and wudna hold oot a false houp tae deceive a sore hert or win escape for himsel'."

"Ye needna plead wi' me, Tammas, to dae the best a' can for yir wife. Man, a' kent her lang afore ye ever luved her; a' brocht her intae the warld, and a' saw her through the fever when she wes a bit lassikie; a' closed her mither's een, and it wes me hed tae tell her she wes an orphan, an' nae man wes better pleased when she got a gude husband, and a' helpit her wi' her fower bairns. A've naither wife nor bairns o' ma own, an' a coont a' the fouk o' the Glen ma family. Div ye think a' wudna save Annie if I cud? If there wes a man in Muirtown 'at cud dae mair for her, a'd have him this verra nicht, but a' the doctors in Perthshire are helpless for this tribble.

"Tammas, ma puir fallow, if it could avail, a' tell ye a' wud lay doon this auld worn-oot ruckle o' a body o' mine juist tae see ye baith sittin' at the fireside, an' the bairns roond ye, couthy an' canty again; but it's no tae be, Tammas, it's no tae be."

"When a' lookit at the doctor's face," Marget said, "a'

Ian Maclaren

thocht him the winsomest man a' ever saw. He wes transfigured that nicht, for a'm judging there's nae transfiguration like luve."

"It's God's wull an' maun be borne, but it's a sair wull for me, an' a'm no ungratefu' tae you, doctor, for a' ye've dune and what ye said the nicht," and Tammas went back to sit with Annie for the last time.

Jess picked her way through the deep snow to the main road, with a skill that came of long experience, and the doctor held converse with her according to his wont.

"Eh, Jess wumman, yon wes the hardest wark a' hae tae face, and a' wud raither hae ta'en ma chance o' anither row in a Glen Urtach drift than tell Tammas Mitchell his wife wes deein'.

"A' said she cudna be cured, and it wes true, for there's juist ae man in the land fit for't, and they micht as weel try tae get the mune oot o' heaven. Sae a' said naethin' tae vex Tammas's hert, for it's heavy eneuch withoot regrets.

"But it's hard, Jess, that money wull buy life after a', an' if Annie wes a duchess her man wudna lose her; but bein' only a puir cottar's wife, she maun dee afore the week's oot.

"Gin we hed him the morn there's little doot she wud be saved, for he hesna lost mair than five per cent, o' his cases, and they 'ill be puir toon's craturs, no strappin' women like Annie.

"It's oot o' the question, Jess, sae hurry up, lass, for we've hed a heavy day. But it wud be the grandest thing that was ever dune in the Glen in oor time if it could be managed by hook or crook.

"We 'ill gang and see Drumsheugh, Jess; he's anither man sin' Geordie Hoo's deith, and he wes aye kinder than fouk kent;" and the doctor passed at a gallop through the village, whose lights shone across the white frost-bound road.

"Come in by, doctor; a' heard ye on the road; ye 'ill hae been at Tammas Mitchell's; hoo's the gudewife? a' doot she's sober."

"Annie's deein', Drumsheugh, an' Tammas is like tae brak his hert."

"That's no lichtsome, doctor, no lichtsome ava, for a' dinna ken ony man in Drumtochty sae bund up in his wife as Tammas, and there's no a bonnier wumman o' her age crosses oor kirk door than Annie, nor a cleverer at her wark. Man, ye 'ill need tae pit yir brains in steep. Is she clean beyond ye?"

"Beyond me and every ither in the land but ane, and it wud cost a hundred guineas tae bring him tae Drumtochty."

"Certes, he's no blate; it's a fell chairge for a short day's work; but hundred or no hundred we 'ill hae him, an' no let Annie gang, and her no half her years."

"Are ye meanin' it, Drumsheugh?" and MacLure turned white below the tan.

"William MacLure," said Drumsheugh, in one of the few confidences that ever broke the Drumtochty

Ian Maclaren

reserve, "a'm a lonely man, wi' naebody o' ma ain blude tae care for me livin', or tae lift me intae ma coffin when a'm deid.

"A' fecht awa at Muirtown market for an extra pund on a beast, or a shillin' on the quarter o' barley, an' what's the gude o't? Burnbrae gaes aff tae get a goon for his wife or a buke for his college laddie, an' Lachlan Campbell 'ill no leave the place noo withoot a ribbon for Flora.

"Ilka man in the Kildrummie train has some bit fairin' in his pooch for the fouk at hame that he's bocht wi' the siller he won.

"But there's naebody tae be lookin' oot for me, an' comin' doon the road tae meet me, and daffin' (joking) wi' me aboot their fairing, or feeling ma pockets. Ou ay, a've seen it a' at ither hooses, though they tried tae hide it frae me for fear a' wud lauch at them. Me lauch, wi' ma cauld, empty hame!

"Yir the only man kens, Weelum, that I aince luved the noblest wumman in the glen or onywhere, an' a' luve her still, but wi' anither luve noo.

"She hed given her heart tae anither, or a've thocht a' micht hae won her, though nae man be worthy o' sic a gift. Ma hert turned tae bitterness, but that passed awa beside the brier bush whar George Hoo lay yon sad simmer time. Some day a'll tell ye ma story, Weelum, for you an' me are auld freends, and will be till we dee."

MacLure felt beneath the table for Drumsheugh's hand, but neither man looked at the other.

"Weel, a' we can dae noo, Weelum, gin we haena mickle brichtness in oor ain hames, is tae keep the licht frae gaein' oot in anither hoose. Write the telegram, man, and Sandy 'ill send it aff frae Kildrurnmie this verra nicht, and ye 'ill hae yir man the morn."

"Yir the man a' coonted ye, Drumsheugh, but ye 'ill grant me ae favour. Ye 'ill lat me pay the half, bit by bit - a' ken yir wullin' tae dae't a', - but a' haena mony pleesures, an' a' wud like tae hae ma ain share in savin' Annie's life."

Next morning a figure received Sir George on the Kildrummie platform, whom that famous surgeon took for a gillie, but who introduced himself as "MacLure of Drumtochty." It seemed as if the East had come to meet the West when these two stood together, the one in travelling furs, handsome and distinguished, with his strong, cultured face and carriage of authority, a characteristic type of his profession; and the other more marvellously dressed than ever, for Drumsheugh's topcoat had been forced upon him for the occasion, his face and neck one redness with the bitter cold; rough and ungainly, yet not without some signs of power in his eye and voice, the most heroic type of his noble profession. MacLure compassed the precious arrival with observances till he was securely seated in Drumsheugh's dogcart - a vehicle that lent itself to history - with two full-sized plaids added to his equipment - Drumsheugh and Hillocks had both been requisitioned - and MacLure wrapped another plaid round a leather case, which was placed below the seat with such reverence as might be given to the Queen's regalia. Peter attended their departure full of interest, and as soon as they were in the fir woods MacLure explained that it would be an eventful journey.

"It's a' richt in here, for the wind disna get at the snaw, but the drifts are deep in the Glen, and th'ill be some engineerin' afore we get tae oor destination."

Four times they left the road and took their way over fields, twice they forced a passage through a slap in a dyke, thrice they used gaps in the paling which MacLure had made on his downward journey.

"A' seleckit the road this mornin', an' a' ken the depth tae an inch; we 'ill get through this steadin' here tae the main road, but oor worst job 'ill be crossin' the Tochty.

"Ye see the bridge hes been shakin' wi' this winter's flood, and we daurna venture on it, sae we hev tae ford, and the snaw's been melting up Urtach way. There's nae doot the water's gey big, and it's threatenin' tae rise, but we 'ill win through wi' a warstle.

"It micht be safer tae lift the instruments oot o' reach o' the water; wud ye mind haddin' them on yir knee till we're ower, an' keep firm in yir seat in case we come on a stane in the bed o' the river."

By this time they had come to the edge, and it was not a cheering sight. The Tochty had spread out over the meadows, and while they waited they could see it cover another two inches on the trunk of a tree. There are summer floods, when the water is brown and flecked with foam, but this was a winter flood, which is black and sullen, and runs in the centre with a strong, fierce, silent current. Upon the op posite side Hillocks stood to give directions by word and hand, as the ford was on his land, and none knew the Tochty better in all its ways.

They passed through the shallow water without mishap, save when the wheel struck a hidden stone or fell suddenly into a rut; but when they neared the body of the river MacLure halted, to give Jess a minute's breathing.

"It 'ill tak ye a' yir time, lass, an' a' wud raither be on yir back; but ye never failed me yet, and a wumman's life is hangin' on the crossin'."

With the first plunge into the bed of the stream the water rose to the axles, and then it crept up to the shafts, so that the surgeon could feel it lapping in about his feet, while the dogcart began to quiver, and it seemed as if it were to be carried away. Sir George was as brave as most men, but he had never forded a Highland river in flood, and the mass of black water racing past beneath, before, behind him, affected his imagination and shook his nerves. He rose from his seat and ordered MacLure to turn back, declaring that he would be condemned utterly and eternally if he allowed himself to be drowned for any person.

"Sit doon," thundered MacLure; "condemned ye will be suner or later gin ye shirk yir duty, but through the water ye gang the day."

Both men spoke much more strongly and shortly, but this is what they intended to say, and it was MacLure that prevailed.

Jess trailed her feet along the ground with cunning art, and held her shoulder against the stream; MacLure leant forward in his seat, a rein in each hand, and his eyes fixed on Hillocks, who was now standing up to the waist in the water, shouting directions and cheering

Ian Maclaren

on horse and driver.

"Haud tae the richt, doctor; there's a hole yonder. Keep oot o't for ony sake. That's it; yir daein' fine. Steady, man, steady. Yir at the deepest; sit heavy in yir seats. Up the channel noo, and ye 'll be oot o' the swirl. Weel dune, Jess, weel dune, auld mare! Mak straicht for me, doctor, an' a'll gie ye the road oot. Ma word, ye've dune yir best, baith o' ye this mornin'," cried Hillocks, splashing up to the dogcart, now in the shallows.

"Sall, it wes titch an' go for a meenut in the middle; a Hielan' ford is a kittle (hazardous) road in the snaw time, but ye're safe noo.

"Gude luck tae ye up at Westerton, sir; nane but a richt-hearted man wud hae riskit the Tochty in flood. Ye're boond tae succeed aifter sic a graund beginning" for it had spread already that a famous surgeon had come to do his best for Annie, Tammas Mitchell's wife.

Two hours later MacLure came out from Annie's room and laid hold of Tammas, a heap of speechless misery by the kitchen fire, and carried him off to the barn, and spread some corn on the threshing floor and thrust a flail into his hands.

"Noo we've tae begin, an' we 'ill no be dune for an' oor, and ye've tae lay on withoot stoppin' till a' come for ye, an' a'll shut the door tae haud in the noise, an' keep yir dog beside ye, for there maunna be a cheep aboot the hoose for Annie's sake."

"A'll dae onythingye want me, but if - if -"

"A'll come for ye, Tammas, gin there be danger; but what are ye feared for wi' the Queen's ain surgeon here?"

Fifty minutes did the flail rise and fall, save twice, when Tammas crept to the door and listened, the dog lifting his head and whining.

It seemed twelve hours instead of one when the door swung back, and MacLure filled the doorway, preceded by a great burst of light, for the sun had arisen on the snow.

His face was as tidings of great joy, and Elspeth told me that there was nothing like it to be seen that afternoon for glory, save the sun itself in the heavens.

"A' never saw the marrow o't, Tammas, an' a'll never see the like again; it's a' ower, man, withoot a hitch frae beginnin' tae end, and she's fa'in' asleep as fine as ye like."

"Dis he think Annie ... 'ill live?"

"Of coorse he dis, and be aboot the hoose inside a month; that's the gude o' bein' a clean-bluided, weel-livin' -"

"Preserve ye, man, what's wrang wi' ye? it's a mercy a' keppit ye, or we wud hev hed anither job for Sir George.

"Ye're a' richt noo; sit doon on the strae. A'll come back in a whilie, an' ye 'ill see Annie juist for a meenut, but ye maunna say a word."

Marget took him in and let him kneel by Annie's bedside.

He said nothing then or afterwards, for speech came only once in his lifetime to Tammas, but Annie whispered, "Ma ain dear man."

When the doctor placed the precious bag beside Sir George in our solitary first next morning, he laid a cheque beside it and was about to leave.

"No, no," said the great man. "Mrs. Macfadyen and I were on the gossip last night, and I know the whole story about you and your friend.

"You have some right to call me a coward, but I'll never let you count me a mean, miserly rascal," and the cheque with Drumsheugh's painful writing fell in fifty pieces on the floor.

As the train began to move, a voice from the first called so that all in the station heard.

"Give's another shake of your hand, MacLure; I'm proud to have met you; you are an honour to our profession. Mind the antiseptic dressings."

It was market day, but only Jamie Soutar and Hillocks had ventured down.

"Did ye hear yon, Hillocks? hoo dae ye feel? A'll no deny a'm lifted"

Halfway to the Junction Hillocks had recovered, and began to grasp the situation.

"Tell's what he said. A' wud like to hae it exact for Drumsheugh."

"Thae's the eedentical words, an' they're true; there's no a man in Drumtochty disna ken that, except ane."

"An' wha's that, Jamie?"

"It's Weelum MacLure himsel. Man, a've often girned that he sud fecht awa for us a', and maybe dee before he kent that he hed githered mair luve than ony man in the Glen.

"'A'm prood tae hae met ye', says Sir George, an' him the greatest doctor in the land. 'Yir an honour tae oor profession.'

"Hillocks, a' wudna hae missed it for twenty notes," said James Soutar, cynic-in-ordinary to the parish of Drumtochty.

III

A FIGHT WITH DEATH

When Drumsheugh's grieve was brought to the gates of death by fever, caught, as was supposed, on an adventurous visit to Glasgow, the London doctor at Lord Kilspindie's shooting lodge looked in on his way from the moor, and declared it impossible for Saunders to live through the night.

"I give him six hours, more or less; it is only a question of time," said the oracle, buttoning his gloves and getting into the brake; "tell your parish doctor that I was sorry not to have met him."

Bell heard this verdict from behind the door, and gave way utterly, but Drumsheugh declined to accept it as final, and devoted himself to consolation.

"Dinna greet like that, Bell wumman, sae lang as Saunders is still livin'; a'll never give up houp, for ma pairt, till oor ain man says the word.

"A' the doctors in the land dinna ken as muckle aboot us as Weelum MacLure, an' he's ill tae beat when he's tryin' tae save a man's life."

MacLure, on his coming, would say nothing, either

weal or woe, till he had examined Saunders. Suddenly his face turned into iron before their eyes, and he looked like one encountering a merciless foe. For there was a feud between MacLure and a certain mighty power which had lasted for forty years in Drumtochty.

"The London doctor said that Saunders wud sough awa afore mornin', did he? Weel, he's an authority on fevers an' sic like diseases, an ought tae ken.

"It's may be presumptous o' me tae differ frae him, and it wudna be verra respectfu' o' Saunders tae live aifter this opeenion. But Saunders wes aye thraun an' ill tae drive, an' he's as like as no tae gang his ain gait.

"A'm no meanin' tae reflect on sae clever a man, but he didna ken the seetuation. He can read fevers like a bulk, but he never cam across sic a thing as the Drumtochty constitution a' his days.

"Ye see, when onybody gets as low as puir Saunders here, it's juist a hand to hand wrastle atween the fever and his constitution, an' of coorse, if he hed been a shilpit, stuntit, feckless effeegy o' a cratur, fed on tea an' made dishes and pushioned wi' bad air, Saunders wud hae nae chance; he wes boond tae gae oot like the snuff o' a candle.

"But Saunders hes been fillin' his lungs for five and thirty year wi' strong Drumtochty air, an' eatin' naethin' but kirny aitmeal, and drinkin' naethin' but fresh milk frae the coo, an' followin' the ploo through the new-turned, sweet-smellin' earth, an' swingin' the scythe in haytime and harvest, till the legs an' airms o' him were iron, an' his chest wes like the cuttin' o' an oak tree.

Ian Maclaren

"He's a waesome sicht the nicht, but Saunders wes a buirdly man aince, and wull never lat his life be taken lichtly frae him. Na, na, he hesna sinned against Nature, and Nature 'ill stand by him noo in his oor o' distress.

"A' daurna say yea, Bell, muckle as a' wud like, for this is an evil disease, cunnin' an' treacherous as the deevil himsel', but a' winna say nay, sae keep yir hert frae despair.

"It wull be a sair fecht, but it 'ill be settled one wy or anither by sax o'clock the morn's morn. Nae man can prophecee hoo it 'ill end, but ae thing is certain, a'll no see deith tak a Drumtochty man afore his time if a' can help it.

"Noo, Bell ma wumman, yir near deid wi' tire, an' nae wonder. Ye've dune a' ye cud for yir man, an' ye 'ill lippen (trust) him the nicht tae Drumsheugh an' me; we 'ill no fail him or you.

"Lie doon an' rest, an' if it be the wull o' the Almichty a'll wauken ye in the mornin' tae see a livin' conscious man, an' if it be itherwise a'll come for ye the suner, Bell," and the big red hand went out to the anxious wife. "A' gie ye ma word."

Bell leant over the bed, and at the sight of Saunders' face a superstitious dread seized her.

"See, doctor, the shadow of deith is on him that never lifts. A've seen it afore, on ma father an' mither. A' canna leave him, a' canna leave him."

"It's hoverin', Bell, but it hesna fallen; please God it

never wull. Gang but and get some sleep, for it's time we were at oor work.

"The doctors in the toons hae nurses an' a' kinds o' handy apparatus," said MacLure to Drumsheugh when Bell had gone, "but you an' me 'ill need tae be nurse the nicht, an' use sic things as we hev.

"It 'ill be a lang nicht and anxious wark, but a' wud raither hae ye, auld freend, wi' me than ony man in the Glen. Ye're no feared tae gie a hand?"

"Me feared? No likely. Man, Saunders cam tae me a haflin, and hes been on Drumsheugh for twenty years, an' though he be a dour chiel, he's a faithfu' servant as ever lived. It's waesome tae see him lyin' there moanin' like some dumb animal frae mornin' tae nicht, an' no able tae answer his ain wife when she speaks.

"Div ye think, Weelum, he hes a chance?"

"That he hes, at ony rate, and it 'ill no be your blame or mine if he hesna mair."

While he was speaking, MacLure took off his coat and waistcoat and hung them on the back of the door. Then he rolled up the sleeves of his shirt and laid bare two arms that were nothing but bone and muscle.

"It gar'd ma very blood rin faster tae the end of ma fingers juist tae look at him," Drumsheugh expatiated afterwards to Hillocks, "for a' saw noo that there was tae be a stand-up fecht atween him an' deith for Saunders, and when a' thocht o' Bell an' her bairns, a' kent wha wud win.

192   Ian Maclaren

"'Aff wi' yir coat, Drumsheugh,' said MacLure; 'ye 'ill need tae bend yir back the nicht; gither a' the pails in the hoose and fill them at the spring, an' a'll come doon tae help ye wi' the carryin'."

It was a wonderful ascent up the steep pathway from the spring to the cottage on its little knoll, the two men in single file, bareheaded, silent, solemn, each with a pail of water in either hand, MacLure limping painfully in front, Drumsheugh blowing behind; and when they laid down their burden in the sick room, where the bits of furniture had been put to a side and a large tub held the centre, Drumsheugh looked curiously at the doctor.

"No, a'm no daft; ye needna be feared; but yir tae get yir first lesson in medicine the nicht, an' if we win the battle ye can set up for yersel in the Glen.

"There's twa dangers - that Saunders' strength fails, an' that the force o' the fever grows; and we have juist twa weapons.

"Yon milk on the drawers' head an' the bottle of whisky is tae keep up the strength, and this cool caller water is tae keep doon the fever.

"We 'ill cast oot the fever by the virtue o' the earth an' the water."

"Div ye mean tae pit Saunders in the tub?"

"Ye hiv it noo, Drumsheugh, and that's hoo a' need yir help."

"Man, Hillocks," Drumsheugh used to moralise, as often as he remembered that critical night, "it wes

humblin' tae see hoo low sickness can bring a pooerfu'
man, an' ocht tae keep us frae pride.

"A month syne there wesna a stronger man in the Glen
than Saunders, an' noo he wes juist a bundle o' skin and
bone, that naither saw nor heard, nor moved nor felt,
that kent naethin' that was dune tae him.

"Hillocks, a' wudna hae wished ony man tae hev seen
Saunders - for it wull never pass frae before ma een as
long as a' live - but a' wish a' the Glen hed stude by
MacLure kneelin' on the floor wi' his sleeves up tae his
oxters and waitin' on Saunders.

"Yon big man wes as pitifu' an' gentle as a wumman,
and when he laid the puir fallow in his bed again, he
happit him ower as a mither dis her bairn."

Thrice it was done, Drumsheugh ever bringing up
colder water from the spring, and twice MacLure was
silent; but after the third time there was a gleam in
his eye.

"We're haudin' oor ain; we're no bein' maistered, at ony
rate; mair a' canna say for three oors.

"We 'ill no need the water again, Drumsheugh; gae oot
and tak a breath o' air; a'm on gaird masel."

It was the hour before daybreak, and Drumsheugh
wandered through fields he had trodden since
childhood. The cattle lay sleeping in the pastures; their
shadowy forms, with a patch of whiteness here and
there, having a weird suggestion of death. He heard the
burn running over the stones; fifty years ago he had
made a dam that lasted till winter. The hooting of an

Ian Maclaren

owl made him start; one had frightened him as a boy so that he ran home to his mother - she died thirty years ago. The smell of ripe corn filled the air; it would soon be cut and garnered. He could see the dim outlines of his house, all dark and cold; no one he loved was beneath the roof. The lighted window in Saunders' cottage told where a man hung between life and death, but love was in that home. The futility of life arose before this lonely man, and overcame his heart with an indescribable sadness. What a vanity was all human labour, what a mystery all human life.

But while he stood, a subtle change came over the night, and the air trembled round him as if one had whispered. Drumsheugh lifted his head and looked eastwards. A faint grey stole over the distant horizon, and suddenly a cloud reddened before his eyes. The sun was not in sight, but was rising, and sending forerunners before his face. The cattle began to stir, a blackbird burst into song, and before Drumsheugh crossed the threshold of Saunders' house, the first ray of the sun had broken on a peak of the Grampians.

MacLure left the bedside, and as the light of the candle fell on the doctor's face, Drumsheugh could see that it was going well with Saunders.

"He's nae waur; an' it's half six noo; it's ower sune tae say mair, but a'm houpin' for the best. Sit doon and take a sleep, for ye're needin' 't, Drumsheugh, an', man, ye hae worked for it"

As he dozed off, the last thing Drumsheugh saw was the doctor sitting erect in his chair, a clenched fist resting on the bed, and his eyes already bright with the vision of victory.

He awoke with a start to find the room flooded with the morning sunshine, and every trace of last night's work removed.

The doctor was bending over the bed, and speaking to Saunders.

"It's me, Saunders, Doctor MacLure, ye ken; dinna try tae speak or move; juist let this drap milk slip ower - ye 'ill be needin' yir breakfast, lad - and gang tae sleep again."

Five minutes, and Saunders had fallen into a deep, healthy sleep, all tossing and moaning come to an end. Then MacLure stepped softly across the floor, picked up his coat and waistcoat, and went out at the door.

Drumsheugh arose and followed him without a word. They passed through the little garden, sparkling with dew, and beside the byre, where Hawkie rattled her chain, impatient for Bell's coming, and by Saunders' little strip of corn ready for the scythe, till they reached an open field. There they came to a halt, and Doctor MacLure for once allowed himself to go.

His coat he flung east and his waistcoat west, as far as he could hurl them, and it was plain he would have shouted had he been a complete mile from Saunders' room. Any less distance was useless for adequate expression. He struck Drumsheugh a mighty blow that well-nigh levelled that substantial man in the dust, and then the doctor of Drumtochty issued his bulletin.

"Saunders wesna tae live through the nicht, but he's livin' this meenut, an' like to live.

Ian Maclaren

"He's got by the warst clean and fair, and wi' him that's as good as cure.

"It' ill be a graund waukenin' for Bell; she 'ill no be a weedow yet, nor the bairnies fatherless.

"There's nae use glowerin' at me, Drumsheugh, for a body's daft at a time, an' a' canna contain masel, and a'm no gaein' tae try."

Then it dawned upon Drumsheugh that the doctor was attempting the Highland fling.

"He's ill made tae begin wi'," Drumsheugh explained in the kirkyard next Sabbath, "and ye ken he's been terrible mishannelled by accidents, sae ye may think what like it wes, but, as sure as deith, o' a' the Hielan' flings a' ever saw yon wes the bonniest.

"A' hevna shaken ma ain legs for thirty years, but a' confess tae a turn masel. Ye may lauch an' ye like, neeburs, but the thocht o' Bell an' the news that wes waitin' her got the better o' me."

Drumtochty did not laugh. Drumtochty looked as if it could have done quite otherwise for joy.

"A' wud hae made a third gin a' hed been there," announced Hillocks, aggressively.

"Come on, Drumsheugh," said Jamie Soutar, "gie's the end o't; it wes a michty mornin'."

"'We're twa auld fules,' says MacLure tae me, and he gaithers up his claithes. 'It wud set us better tae be tellin' Bell.'

"She wes sleepin' on the top o' her bed wrapped in a plaid, fair worn oot wi' three weeks' nursin' o' Saunders, but at the first touch she was oot upon the floor.

"'Is Saunders deein', doctor?' she cries. 'Ye promised tae wauken me; dinna tell me it's a' ower.'

"'There's nae deein' aboot him, Bell; ye're no tae lose yir man this time, sae far as a' can see. Come ben an' jidge for yersel'.

"Bell lookit at Saunders, and the tears of joy fell on the bed like rain.

"'The shadow's lifted,' she said; 'he's come back frae the mooth o' the tomb.

"'A' prayed last nicht that the Lord wud leave Saunders till the laddies cud dae for themselves, an' thae words came intae ma mind, "Weepin' may endure for a nicht, but joy cometh in the mornin'."

"'The Lord heard ma prayer, and joy hes come in the mornin', an' she gripped the doctor's hand.

"'Ye've been the instrument, Doctor MacLure. Ye wudna gie him up, and ye did what nae ither cud for him, an' a've ma man the day, and the bairns hae their father.'

"An' afore MacLure kent what she was daein', Bell lifted his hand to her lips an' kissed it."

"Did she, though?" cried Jamie. "Wha wud hae thocht there wes as muckle spunk in Bell?"

"MacLure, of coorse, was clean scandalised," continued Drumsheugh, "an' pooed awa his hand as if it hed been burned.

"Nae man can thole that kind o' fraikin', and a' never heard o' sic a thing in the parish, but we maun excuse Bell, neeburs; it wes an occasion by ordinar," and Drumsheugh made Bell's apology to Drumtochty for such an excess of feeling.

"A' see naethin' tae excuse," insisted Jamie, who was in great fettle that Sabbath; "the doctor hes never been burdened wi' fees, and a'm judgin' he coonted a wumman's gratitude that he saved frae weedowhood the best he ever got."

"A' gaed up tae the Manse last nicht," concluded Drumsheugh, "and telt the minister hoo the doctor focht aucht oors for Saunders' life, an' won, and ye never saw a man sae carried. He walkit up and doon the room a' the time, and every other meenut he blew his nose like a trumpet.

"'I've a cold in my head to-night, Drumsheugh,' says he; 'never mind me.'"

"A've hed the same masel in sic circumstances; they come on sudden," said Jamie.

"A' wager there 'ill be a new bit in the laist prayer the day, an' somethin' worth hearin'."

And the fathers went into kirk in great expectation.

"We beseech Thee for such as be sick, that Thy hand may be on them for good, and that Thou wouldst restore them again to health and strength," was the familiar petition of every Sabbath.

The congregation waited in a silence that might be heard, and were not disappointed that morning, for the minister continued:

"Especially we tender Thee hearty thanks that Thou didst spare Thy servant who was brought down into the dust of death, and hast given him back to his wife and children, and unto that end didst wonderfully bless the skill of him who goes out and in amongst us, the beloved physician of this parish and adjacent districts."

"Didna a' tell ye, neeburs?" said Jamie, as they stood at the kirkyard gate before dispersing; "there's no a man in the coonty cud hae dune it better. 'Beloved physician,' an' his 'skill,' tae, an' bringing in 'adjacent districts'; that's Glen Urtach; it wes handsome, and the doctor earned it, ay, every word.

"It's an awfu' peety he didna hear yon; but dear knows whar he is the day, maist likely up -"

Jamie stopped suddenly at the sound of a horse's feet, and there, coming down the avenue of beech trees that made a long vista from the kirk gate, they saw the doctor and Jess.

One thought flashed through the minds of the fathers of the commonwealth.

It ought to be done as he passed, and it would be done if it were not Sabbath. Of course it was out of the question on Sabbath.

The doctor is now distinctly visible, riding after his fashion.

There was never such a chance, if it were only Saturday; and each man reads his own regret in his neighbour's face.

The doctor is nearing them rapidly; they can imagine the shepherd's tartan.

Sabbath or no Sabbath, the Glen cannot let him pass without some tribute of their pride.

Jess has recognised friends, and the doctor is drawing rein.

"It hes tae be dune," said Jamie desperately, "say what ye like." Then they all looked towards him, and Jamie led.

"Hurrah," swinging his Sabbath hat in the air, "hurrah," and once more, "hurrah," Whinnie Knowe, Drumsheugh, and Hillocks joining lustily, but Tammas Mitchell carrying all before him, for he had found at last an expression for his feelings that rendered speech unnecessary.

It was a solitary experience for horse and rider, and Jess bolted without delay. But the sound followed and surrounded them, and as they passed the corner of the kirkyard, a figure waved his college cap over the wall and gave a cheer on his own account.

"God bless you, doctor, and well done."

" If it isna the minister," cried Drumsheugh, "in his

goon an' bans; tae think o' that; but a' respeck him for it."

Then Drumtochty became self-conscious, and went home in confusion of face and unbroken silence, except Jamie Soutar, who faced his neighbours at the parting of the ways without shame.

"A' wud dae it a' ower again if a' hed the chance; he got naethin' but his due."

It was two miles before Jess composed her mind, and the doctor and she could discuss it quietly together.

"A' can hardly believe ma ears, Jess, an' the Sabbath tae; their verra jidgment hes gane frae the fouk o' Drumtochty.

"They've heard about Saunders, a'm thinkin', wumman, and they're pleased we brocht him roond; he's fairly on the mend, ye ken, noo.

"A' never expeckit the like o' this, though, and it wes juist a wee thingie mair than a' cud hae stude.

"Ye hev yir share in't tae, lass; we've hed mony a hard nicht and day thegither, an' yon wes oor reward. No mony men in this warld 'ill ever get a better, for it cam frae the hert o' honest fouk."

Ian Maclaren

IV

THE DOCTOR'S LAST JOURNEY

Drumtochty had a vivid recollection of the winter when Dr. MacLure was laid up for two months with a broken leg, and the Glen was dependent on the dubious ministrations of the Kildrummie doctor. Mrs. Macfadyen also pretended to recall a "whup" of some kind or other he had in the fifties, but this was considered to be rather a pyrotechnic display of Elspeth's superior memory than a serious statement of fact. MacLure could not have ridden through the snow of forty winters without suffering, yet no one ever heard him complain, and he never pled illness to any messenger by night or day.

"It took me," said Jamie Soutar to Milton afterwards, "the feck o' ten meenuts tae howk him an' Jess oot ae snawy nicht when Drums turned bad sudden, and if he didna try to excuse himself for no hearing me at aince wi' some story aboot juist comin' in frae Glen Urtach, and no bein' in his bed for the laist twa nichts.

"He wes that carefu' o' himsel an' lazy that if it hedna been for the siller, a've often thocht, Milton, he wud never hae dune a handstroke o' wark in the Glen.

"What scunnered me wes the wy the bairns were ta'en

in wi' him. Man, a've seen him tak a wee laddie on his knee that his ain mither cudna quiet, an' lilt 'Sing a song o' saxpence' till the bit mannie wud be lauchin' like a gude ane, an' pooin' the doctor's beard.

"As for the weemen, he fair cuist a glamour ower them; they're daein' naethin' noo but speak aboot this body and the ither he cured, an' hoo he aye hed a couthy word for sick fouk. Weemen hae nae discernment, Milton; tae hear them speak ye wud think MacLure hed been a releegious man like yersel, although, as ye said, he wes little mair than a Gallic.

"Bell Baxter was haverin' awa in the shop tae sic an extent aboot the wy MacLure brocht roond Saunders when he hed the fever that a' gied oot at the door, a wes that disgusted, an' a'm telt when Tammas Mitchell heard the news in the smiddy he wes juist on the greeting.

"The smith said that he wes thinkin' o' Annie's tribble, but ony wy a' ca' it rael bairnly. It's no like Drumtochty; ye're setting an example, Milton, wi' yir composure. But a' mind ye took the doctor's meesure as sune as ye cam intae the pairish."

It is the penalty of a cynic that he must have some relief for his secret grief, and Milton began to weary of life in Jamie's hands during those days.

Drumtochty was not observant in the matter of health, but they had grown sensitive about Dr. MacLure, and remarked in the kirkyard all summer that he was failing.

"He wes aye spare," said Hillocks, "an' he's been sair

twisted for the laist twenty year, but a' never mind him booed till the year. An' he's gaein' intae sma' buke (bulk), an' a' dinna like that, neeburs.

"The Glen wudna dae weel withoot Weelum MacLure, an' he's no as young as he wes. Man, Drumsheugh, ye micht wile him aff tae the saut water atween the neeps and the hairst. He's been workin' forty year for a holiday, an' it's aboot due."

Drumsheugh was full of tact, and met MacLure quite by accident on the road.

"Saunders 'ill no need me till the shearing begins," he explained to the doctor, "an' a'm gaein' tae Brochty for a turn o' the hot baths; they're fine for the rheumatics.

"Wull ye no come wi' me for auld lang syne? it's lonesome for a solitary man, an' it wud dae ye gude."

"Na, na, Drumsheugh," said MacLure, who understood perfectly, "a've dune a' thae years withoot a break, an' a'm laith (unwilling) tae be takin' holidays at the tail end.

"A'll no be mony months wi' ye a' thegither noo, an' a'm wanting tae spend a' the time a' hev in the Glen. Ye see yersel that a'll sune be getting ma lang rest, an' a'll no deny that a'm wearyin' for it."

As autumn passed into winter, the Glen noticed that the doctor's hair had turned grey, and that his manner had lost all its roughness. A feeling of secret gratitude filled their hearts, and they united in a conspiracy of attention. Annie Mitchell knitted a huge comforter in red and white, which the doctor wore in misery for one whole day, out of respect for Annie, and then hung in his sitting-room as a wall ornament. Hillocks used to intercept him with hot drinks, and one drifting day compelled him to shelter till the storm abated. Flora Campbell brought a wonderful compound of honey and whisky, much tasted in Auchindarroch, for his cough, and the mother of young Burnbrae filled his cupboard with black jam, as a healing measure. Jamie Soutar seemed to have an endless series of jobs in the doctor's direction, and looked in "juist tae rest himsel" in the kitchen.

MacLure had been slowly taking in the situation, and at last he unburdened himself one night to Jamie.

"What ails the fouk, think ye? for they're aye lecturin' me noo tae tak care o' the weet and tae wrap masel up, an' there's no a week but they're sendin' bit presents tae the hoose, till a'm fair ashamed."

"Oo, a'll explain that in a meenut," answered Jamie, "for a' ken the Glen weel. Ye see they're juist tryin' the Scripture plan o' heapin' coals o' fire on yer head.

"Here ye've been negleckin' the fouk in seeckness an' lettin' them dee afore their freends' eyes withoot a fecht, an' refusin' tae gang tae a puir wumman in her tribble, an' frichtenin' the bairns - no, a'm no dune - and scourgin' us wi' fees, and livin' yersel on the fat o' the land.

"Ye've been carryin' on this trade ever sin yir father dee'd, and the Glen didna notis. But ma word, they've fund ye oot at laist, an' they're gaein' tae mak ye suffer for a' yir ill usage. Div ye understand noo?" said Jamie, savagely.

For a while MacLure was silent, and then he only said:

"It's little a' did for the puir bodies; but ye hev a gude hert, Jamie, a rael good hert."

It was a bitter December Sabbath, and the fathers were settling the affairs of the parish ankle deep in snow, when MacLure's old housekeeper told Drumsheugh that the doctor was not able to rise, and wished to see him in the afternoon.

"Ay, ay," said Hillocks, shaking his head, and that day Drumsheugh omitted four pews with the ladle, while Jamie was so vicious on the way home that none could endure him.

Janet had lit a fire in the unused grate, and hung a plaid by the window to break the power of the cruel north wind, but the bare room with its half-a-dozen bits of furniture and a worn strip of carpet, and the outlook upon the snow drifted up to the second pane of the window and the black firs laden with their icy burden, sent a chill to Drumsheugh's heart.

The doctor had weakened sadly, and could hardly lift his head, but his face lit up at the sight of his visitor, and the big hand, which was now quite refined in its whiteness, came out from the bed-clothes with the old warm grip.

"Come in by, man, and sit doon; it's an awfu' day tae bring ye sae far, but a' kent ye wudna grudge the traivel.

"A' wesna sure till last nicht, an' then a' felt it wudna be lang, an' a' took a wearyin' this mornin' tae see ye.

"We've been freends sin' we were laddies at the auld schule in the firs, an' a' wud like ye tae be wi' me at the end. Ye 'ill stay the nicht, Paitrick, for auld lang syne."

Drumsheugh was much shaken, and the sound of the Christian name, which he had not heard since his mother's death, gave him a "grue" (shiver), as if one had spoken from the other world.

"It's maist awfu' tae hear ye speakin' aboot deein', Weelum; a' canna bear it. We 'ill hae the Muirtown doctor up, an' ye 'ill be aboot again in nae time.

"Ye hevna ony sair tribble; ye're juist trachled wi' hard wark an' needin' a rest. Dinna say ye're gaein' tae leave us, Weelum; we canna dae withoot ye in Drumtochty;" and Drumsheugh looked wistfully for some word of hope.

"Na, na, Paitrick, naethin' can be dune, an' it's ower late tae send for ony doctor. There's a knock that canna be mista'en, an' a' heard it last night. A've focht deith for ither fouk mair than forty year, but ma ain time hes come at laist.

"A've nae tribble worth mentionin' - a bit titch o' bronchitis - an' a've hed a graund constitution; but a'm fair worn oot, Paitrick; that's ma complaint, an' its past curin'."

Drumsheugh went over to the fireplace, and for a while did nothing but break up the smouldering peats, whose smoke powerfully affected his nose and eyes.

"When ye're ready, Paitrick, there's twa or three little trokes a' wud like ye tae look aifter , an' a'll tell ye aboot them as lang's ma head's clear.

"A' didna keep buiks, as ye ken, for a' aye hed a guid memory, so naebody 'ill be harried for money aifter ma deith, and ye 'ill hae nae accoonts tae collect.

"But the fouk are honest in Drumtochty, and they 'ill be offerin' ye siller, an' a'll gie ye ma mind aboot it. Gin it be a puir body, tell her tae keep it and get a bit plaidie wi' the money, and she 'ill maybe think o' her auld doctor at a time. Gin it be a bien (well-to-do) man, tak half of what he offers, for a Drumtochty man wud scorn to be mean in sic circumstances; and if onybody needs a doctor an' canna pay for him, see he's no left tae dee when a'm oot o' the road."

"Nae fear o' that as lang as a'm living Weelum; that hundred's still tae the fore, ye ken, an' a'll tak care it's weel spent.

" Yon wes the best job we ever did thegither, an' dookin' Saunders; ye 'ill no forget that nicht, Weelum" - a gleam came into the doctor's eyes - "tae say naethin' o' the Highlan' fling."

The remembrance of that great victory came upon Drumsheugh, and tried his fortitude.

"What 'ill become o's when ye're no here tae gie a hand in time o' need? we 'ill tak ill wi' a stranger that disna ken ane o's frae anither."

"It's a' for the best, Paitrick, an' ye 'ill see that in a whilie. A've kent fine that ma day wes ower, an' that ye sud hae a younger man.

"A' did what a' cud tae keep up wi' the new medicine, but a' hed little time for readin', an' nane for traivellin'.

"A'm the last o' the auld schule, an' a' ken as weel as onybody thet a' wesna sae dainty an' fine-mannered as the town doctors. Ye took me as a' wes, an' naebody ever cuist up tae me that a' wes a plain man. Na, na; ye've been rael kind an' conseederate a' thae years."

"Weelum, gin ye cairry on sic nonsense ony langer," interrupted Drumsheugh, huskily, "a'll leave the hoose; a' canna stand it."

"It's the truth, Paitrick, but we 'ill gae on wi' our wark, for a'm failin' fast.

"Gie Janet ony sticks of furniture she needs tae furnish a hoose, and sell a' thing else tae pay the wricht (undertaker) an' bedrel (grave-digger). If the new doctor be a young laddie and no verra rich, ye micht let him hae the buiks an' instruments; it 'ill aye be a help.

"But a' wudna like ye tae sell Jess, for she's been a faithfu' servant, an' a' freend tae. There's a note or twa in that drawer a' savit, an' if ye kent ony man that wud gie her a bite o' grass and a sta' in his stable till she followed her maister -"

"Confoond ye, Weelum," broke out Drumsheugh; "its doonricht cruel o' ye to speak like this tae me. Whar wud Jess gang but tae Drumsheugh? she 'ill hae her run o' heck an' manger sae lang as she lives; the Glen wudna like tae see anither man on Jess, and nae man 'ill ever touch the auld mare."

"Dinna mind me, Paitrick, for a' expeckit this; but ye

210   Ian Maclaren

ken we're no verra gleg wi' oor tongues in Drumtochty, an' dinna tell a' that's in oor hearts.

"Weel, that's a' that a' mind, an' the rest a' leave tae yersel'. A've neither kith nor kin tae bury me, sae you an' the neeburs 'ill need tae lat me doon; but gin Tammas Mitchell or Saunders be stannin' near and lookin' as if they wud like a cord, gie't tae them, Paitrick. They're baith dour chiels, and haena muckle tae say, but Tammas lies a graund hert, and there's waur fouk in the Glen than Saunders.

"A'm gettin' drowsy, an' a'll no be able tae follow ye sune, a' doot; wud ye read a bit tae me afore a' fa' ower?

"Ye 'ill find ma mither's Bible on the drawers' heid, but ye 'ill need tae come close tae the bed, for a'm no hearin' or seein' sae weel as a' wes when ye cam."

Drumsheugh put on his spectacles and searched for a comfortable Scripture, while the light of the lamp fell on his shaking hands and the doctor's face, where the shadow was now settling.

"Ma mither aye wantit this read tae her when she wes sober" (weak), and Drumsheugh began, "In My Father's house are many mansions," but MacLure stopped him.

"It's a bonnie word, an' yir mither wes a sanct; but it's no for the like o' me. It's ower gude; a' daurna tak it.

"Shut the buik an' let it open itsel, an' ye 'ill get a bit a've been readin' every nicht the laist month."

Then Drumsheugh found the Parable wherein the Master tells us what God thinks of a Pharisee and of a penitent sinner, till he came to the words: "And the publican, standing afar off, would not lift up so much as his eyes to heaven, but smote upon his breast, saying, God be merciful to me a sinner."

"That micht hae been written for me, Paitrick, or ony ither auld sinner that hes feenished his life, an' hes naethin' tae say for himsel'.

"It wesna easy for me tae get tae kirk, but a' cud hae managed wi' a stretch, an' a' used langidge a' sudna, an' a' micht hae been gentler, and no been so short in the temper. A' see't a' noo.

"It's ower late tae mend, but ye 'ill maybe juist say to the fouk that I wes sorry, an' a'm houpin' that the Almichty 'ill hae mercy on me.

"Cud ye ... pit up a bit prayer, Paitrick?"

"A' haena the words," said Drumsheugh in great distress; "wud ye like's tae send for the minister?"

"It's no the time for that noo, an' a' wud rather hae yersel' - juist what's in yir heart, Paitrick: the Almichty 'ill ken the lave (rest) Himsel'."

So Drumsheugh knelt and prayed with many pauses.

"Almichty God ... dinna be hard on Weelum MacLure, for he's no been hard wi' onybody in Drumtochty.... Be kind tae him as he's been tae us a' for forty year.... We're a' sinners afore Thee.... Forgive him what he's dune wrang, an' dinna cuist it up tae him.... Mind the

fouk he's helpit ... the weemen an' bairnies ... an' gie
him a welcome name, for he's sair needin't after a' his
wark.... Amen."

"Thank ye, Paitrick, and gude nicht tae ye. Ma ain true
freend, gie's yir hand, for a'll maybe no ken ye again.

"Noo a'll say ma mither's prayer and hae a sleep, but ye
'ill no leave me till a' is ower."

Then he repeated as he had done every night of his life:

> "This night I lay me down to sleep,
> I pray the Lord my soul to keep,
> And if I die before I wake,
> I pray the Lord my soul to take."

He was sleeping quietly when the wind drove the snow
against the window with a sudden "swish ;" and he
instantly awoke, so to say, in his sleep. Some one
needed him.

"Are ye frae Glen Urtach?" and an unheard voice
seemed to have answered him.

"Worse is she, an' sufferin' awfu'; that's no lichtsome;
ye did richt tae come.

"The front door's drifted up; gang roond tae the back,
an' ye 'ill get intae the kitchen; a'll be ready in a
meenut.

"Gie's a hand wi' the lantern when a'm saidling Jess,
an' ye needna come on till daylicht; a' ken the road."

Then he was away in his sleep on some errand of

mercy, and struggling through the storm.

"It's a coorse nicht, Jess, an' heavy traivellin'; can ye see afore ye, lass? for a'm clean confused wi' the snaw; bide a wee till a' find the diveesion o' the roads; it's aboot here back or forrit.

"Steady, lass, steady, dinna plunge; it's a drift we're in, but ye're no sinkin'; ... up noo; ... there ye are on the road again.

"Eh, it's deep the nicht, an' hard on us baith, but there's a puir wumman micht dee if we didna warstle through; that's it; ye ken fine what a'm sayin'.

"We 'ill hae tae leave the road here, an' tak tae the muir. Sandie 'ill no can leave the wife alane tae meet us; ... feel for yersel', lass, and keep oot o' the holes.

"Yon's the hoose black in the snaw. Sandie! man, ye frichtened us; a' didna see ye ahint the dyke; hoo's the wife?"

After a while he began again:

"Ye're fair dune, Jess, and so a' am masel'; we're baith gettin' auld, an' dinna tak sae weel wi' the nicht wark.

"We 'ill sune be hame noo; this is the black wood, and it's no lang aifter that; we're ready for oor beds, Jess; ... ay, ye like a clap at a time; mony a mile we've gaed hegither.

"Yon's the licht in the kitchen window; nae wonder ye're nickering (neighing); ... it's been a stiff journey; a'm tired, lass ... a'm tired tae deith," and the voice died into silence.

Drumsheugh held his friend's hand, which now and again tightened in his, and as he watched, a change came over the face on the pillow beside him. The lines of weariness disappeared, as if God's hand had passed over it; and peace began to gather round the closed eyes.

The doctor has forgotten the toil of later years, and has gone back to his boyhood.

"The Lord's my Shepherd, I'll not want,"

he repeated, till he came to the last verse, and then he hesitated.

"Goodness and mercy all my life
Shall surely follow me.

"Follow me ... and ... and ... what's next? Mither said I wes tae haed ready when she cam.

"'A'll come afore ye gang tae sleep, Wullie, but ye 'ill no get yir kiss unless ye can feenish the psalm.'

"And ... in God's house ... for evermore my ... hoo dis it rin? a' canna mind the next word ... my, my -

"It's ower dark noo tae read it, an' mither 'ill sune be comin'."

Drumsheugh, in an agony, whispered into his ear, "'My dwelling-place,' Weelum."

"That's it, that's it a' noo; wha said it?

> "And in God's house for evermore
> My dwelling-place shall be.

"A'm ready noo, an' a'll get ma kiss when mither comes; a' wish she wud come, for a'm tired an' wantin' tae sleep.

"Yon's her step ... an' she's carryin' a licht in her hand; a' see it through the door.

"Mither! a' kent ye wudna forget yir laddie, for ye promised tae come, and a've feenished ma psalm.

> "And in God's house for evermore
> My dwelling-place shall be.

"Gie me the kiss, mither, for a've been waitin' for ye, an' a'll sune be asleep."

The grey morning light fell on Drumsheugh, still holding his friend's cold hand, and staring at a hearth where the fire had died down into white ashes; but the peace on the doctor's face was of one who rested from his labours.

Ian Maclaren

V

THE MOURNING OF THE GLEN

Dr. MacLure was buried during the great snowstorm, which is still spoken of, and will remain the standard of snowfall in Drumtochty for the century. The snow was deep on the Monday, and the men that gave notice of his funeral had hard work to reach the doctor's distant patients. On Tuesday morning it began to fall again in heavy fleecy flakes, and continued till Thursday, and then on Thursday the north wind rose and swept the snow into the hollows of the roads that went to the upland farms, and built it into a huge bank at the mouth of Glen Urtach, and laid it across our main roads in drifts of every size and the most lovely shapes, and filled up crevices in the hills to the depth of fifty feet.

On Friday morning the wind had sunk to passing gusts that powdered your coat with white, and the sun was shining on one of those winter landscapes no towns-man can imagine and no countryman ever forgets. The Glen, from end to end and side to side, was clothed in a glistering mantle white as no fuller on earth could white it, that flung its skirts over the clumps of trees and scattered farm-houses, and was only divided where the Tochty ran with black, swollen stream. The great moor rose and fell in swelling billows of snow that arched themselves over the burns, running deep in the mossy ground, and hid the black peat bogs with a thin, treacherous crust. Beyond, the hills northwards and westwards stood high in white majesty, save where the black crags of Glen Urtach broke the line, and, above our lower Grampians, we caught glimpses of the distant peaks that lifted their heads in holiness unto God.

It seemed to me a fitting day for William MacLure's funeral, rather than summer time, with its flowers and golden corn. He had not been a soft man, nor had he lived an easy life, and now he was to be laid to rest amid the austere majesty of winter, yet in the shining of the sun. Jamie Soutar, with whom I toiled across the Glen, did not think with me, but was gravely concerned.

"Nae doot it's a graund sicht; the like o't is no gien tae us twice in a generation, an' nae king wes ever carried tae his tomb in sic a cathedral.

"But it's the fouk a'm conseederin', an' hoo they 'ill win through; it's hard eneuch for them 'at's on the road, an' it's clean impossible for the lave.

"They 'ill dae their best, every man o' them, ye may depend on that, an' hed it been open weather there wudna hev been six able-bodied men missin'.

"A' wes mad at them, because they never said onything when he wes leevin', but they felt for a' that what he hed dune, an', a' think, he kent it afore he deed.

"He hed juist ae faut, tae ma thinkin', for a' never jidged the waur o' him for his titch of rochness - guid

Ian Maclaren

trees hae gnarled bark - but he thocht ower little o' himsel.

"Noo, gin a' hed asked him hoo mony fouk wud come tae his beerial, he wud hae said, 'They 'ill be Drumsheugh an' yersel', an' maybe twa or three neeburs besides the minister,' an' the fact is that nae man in oor time wud hae sic a githerin' if it werena for the storm.

"Ye see," said Jamie, who had been counting heads all morning, "there's six shepherds in Glen Urtach - they're shut up fast; an' there micht hae been a gude half dizen frae Dunleith wy, an' a'm telt there's nae road; an' there's the heich Glen, nae man cud cross the muir the day, an' it's aucht mile roond;" and Jamie proceeded to review the Glen in every detail of age, driftiness of road and strength of body, till we arrived at the doctor's cottage, when he had settled on a reduction of fifty through stress of weather.

Drumsheugh was acknowledged as chief mourner by the Glen, and received us at the gate with a labored attempt at everyday manners.

"Ye've hed heavy traivellin', a' doot, an' ye 'ill be cauld. It's hard weather for the sheep, an' a'm thinkin' this 'ill be a feeding storm.

"There wes nae use trying tae dig oot the front door yestreen, for it wud hae been drifted up again before morning. We've cleared awa the snow at the back for the prayer; ye 'ill get in at the kitchen door.

"There's a puckle Dunleith men -"

"Wha?" cried Jamie in an instant.

"Dunleith men," said Drumsheugh.

"Div ye mean they're here, whar are they?"

"Drying themsels at the fire, an' no withoot need; ane of them gied ower the head in a drift, and his neeburs hed tae pu' him oot.

"It took them a gude fower oors tae get across, an' it wes coorse wark; they likit him weel doon that wy, an', Jamie man" - here Drumsheugh's voice changed its note, and his public manner disappeared - "what div ye think o' this? every man o' them hes on his blacks."

"It's mair than cud be expeckit," said Jamie; "but whar dae yon men come frae, Drumsheugh?"

Two men in plaids were descending the hill behind the doctor's cottage, taking three feet at a stride, and carrying long staffs in their hands.

"They're Glen Urtach men, Jamie, for ane o' them wes at Kildrummie fair wi' sheep, but hoo they've wun doon passes me."

"It canna be, Drumsheugh," said Jamie, greatly excited. "Glen Urtach's steikit up wi' sna like a locked door.

"Ye're no surely frae the Glen, lads?" as the men leaped the dyke and crossed to the back door, the snow falling from their plaids as they walked.

"We're that an' nae mistak, but a' thocht we wud be

lickit ae place, eh, Chairlie? a'm no sae weel acquant wi' the hill on this side, an' there wes some kittle (hazardous) drifts."

"It wes grand o' ye tae mak the attempt," said Drumsheugh, "an' a'm gled ye're safe."

"He cam through as bad himsel tae help ma wife," was Charlie's reply.

"They're three mair Urtach shepherds 'ill come in by sune; they're frae Upper Urtach, an' we saw them fording the river; ma certes, it took them a' their time, for it wes up tae their waists and rinnin' like a mill lade, but they jined hands and cam ower fine." And the Urtach men went in to the fire.

The Glen began to arrive in twos and threes, and Jamie, from a point of vantage at the gate, and under an appearance of utter indifference, checked his roll till even he was satisfied.

"Weelum MacLure 'ill hae the beerial he deserves in spite o' sna and drifts; it passes a' tae see hoo they've githered frae far an' near.

"A'm thinkin'ye can colleck them for the minister noo, Drumsheugh. A'body's here except the heich Glen, an' we mauna hike for them."

"Dinna be sae sure o' that, Jamie. Yon's terrible like them on the road, wi' Whinnie at their head;" and so it was, twelve in all, only old Adam Ross absent, detained by force, being eighty-two years of age.

"It wud hae been temptin' Providence tae cross the

muir," Whinnie explained, "and it's a fell stap roond; a' doot we're laist."

"See, Jamie," said Drumsheugh, as he went to the house, "gin there be ony antern body in sicht afore we begin; we maun mak allooances the day wi' twa feet o' sna on the grund, tae say naethin' o' drifts."

"There's something at the turnin', an' it's no fouk; it's a machine o' some kind or ither - maybe a bread cart that's focht its wy up."

"Na, it's no that; there's twa horses, ane afore the ither; if it's no a dogcairt wi' twa men in the front; they 'ill be comin' tae the beerial."

"What wud ye sae, Jamie," Hillocks suggested, "but it micht be some o' thae Muirtown doctors? they were awfu' chief wi' MacLure."

"It's nae Muirtown doctors," cried Jamie, in great exultation, "nor ony ither doctors. A' ken thae horses, and wha's ahint them. Quick, man Hillocks, stop the fouk, and tell Drumsheugh tae come oot, for Lord Kilspindie hes come up frae Muirtown Castle."

Jamie himself slipped behind, and did not wish to be seen.

"It's the respeck he's gettin' the day frae high an' low," was Jamie's husky apology; "tae think o' them fechtin' their wy doon frae Glen Urtach, and toiling roond frae the heich Glen, an' his lordship driving through the drifts a' the road frae Muirtown, juist tae honour Weelum MacLure's beerial.

Ian Maclaren

"It's nae ceremony the day, ye may lippen tae it; it's the hert brocht the fouk, an' ye can see it in their faces; ilka man hes his ain reason, an' he's thinkin' on't, though he's speakin' o' naethin' but the storm; he's mindin' the day Weelum pued him oot frae the jaws o' death, or the nicht he savit the gude wife in her oor o' tribble.

"That's why they pit on their blacks this mornin' afore it wes licht, and wrastled through the sna drifts at risk o' life. Drumtochty fouk canna say muckle, it's an awfu' peety, and they 'ill dae their best tae show naethin', but a' can read it a' in their een.

"But wae's me" - and Jamie broke down utterly behind a fir tree, so tender a thing is a cynic's heart - "that fouk 'ill tak a man's best wark a' his days withoot a word an' no dae him honour till he dees. Oh, if they hed only githered like this juist aince when he wes livin', an' lat him see he hedna laboured in vain. His reward hes come ower late, ower late."

During Jamie's vain regret, the Castle trap, bearing the marks of a wild passage in the snow-covered wheels, a broken shaft tied with rope, a twisted lamp, and the panting horses, pulled up between two rows of farmers, and Drumsheugh received his lordship with evident emotion.

"Ma lord ... we never thocht o' this ... an' sic a road."

"How are you, Drumsheugh? and how are you all this wintry day? That's how I'm half an hour late; it took us four hours' stiff work for sixteen miles, mostly in the drifts, of course."

"It wes gude o' yir lordship, tae mak sic an effort, an'

the hale Glen wull be gratefu' tae ye, for ony kindness tae him is kindness tae us."

"You make too much of it, Drumsheugh," and the clear, firm voice was heard of all; "it would have taken more than a few snow drifts to keep me from showing my respect to William MacLure's memory."

When all had gathered in a half circle before the kitchen door, Lord Kilspindie came out - every man noticed he had left his overcoat, and was in black, like the Glen - and took a place in the middle with Drumsheugh and Burnbrae, his two chief tenants, on the right and left, and as the minister appeared every man bared his head.

The doctor looked on the company - a hundred men such as for strength and gravity you could hardly have matched in Scotland - standing out in picturesque relief against the white background, and he said:

"It's a bitter day, friends, and some of you are old; perhaps it might be wise to cover your heads before I begin to pray."

Lord Kilspindie, standing erect and greyheaded between the two old men, replied:

"We thank you, Dr. Davidson, for your thoughtfulness; but he endured many a storm in our service, and we are not afraid of a few minutes' cold at his funeral."

A look flashed round the stern faces, and was reflected from the minister, who seemed to stand higher.

His prayer, we noticed with critical appreciation, was

224   Ian Maclaren

composed for the occasion, and the first part was a thanksgiving to God for the life-work of our doctor, wherein each clause was a reference to his services and sacrifices. No one moved or said Amen - it had been strange with us - but when every man had heard the gratitude of his dumb heart offered to Heaven, there was a great sigh.

After which the minister prayed that we might have grace to live as this man had done from youth to old age, not for himself, but for others, and that we might be followed to our grave by somewhat of "that love wherewith we mourn this day Thy servant departed." Again the same sigh, and the minister said Amen.

The "wricht" stood in the doorway without speaking, and four stalwart men came forward. They were the volunteers that would lift the coffin and carry it for the first stage. One was Tammas, Annie Mitchell's man; and another was Saunders Baxter, for whose life MacLure had his great fight with death; and the third was the Glen Urtach shepherd for whose wife's sake MacLure suffered a broken leg and three fractured ribs in a drift; and the fourth, a Dunleith man, had his own reasons of remembrance.

"He's far lichter than ye wud expeck for sae big a man - there wesna muckle left o' him, ye see - but the road is heavy, and a'll change ye aifter the first half mile."

"Ye needna tribble yersel, wricht," said the man from Glen Urtach; "the'll be nae change in the cairryin' the day," and Tammas was thankful some one had saved him speaking.

Surely no funeral is like unto that of a doctor for pathos, and a peculiar sadness fell on that company as his body was carried out who for nearly half a century had been their help in sickness, and had beaten back death time after time from their door. Death after all was victor, for the man that saved them had not been able to save himself.

As the coffin passed the stable door a horse neighed within, and every man looked at his neighbour. It was his old mare crying to her master.

Jamie slipped into the stable, and went up into the stall.

"Puir lass, ye're no gaein' wi' him the day, an' ye 'ill never see him again; ye've hed yir last ride thegither, an' ye were true tae the end."

After the funeral Drumsheugh came himself for Jess, and took her to his farm. Saunders made a bed for her with soft, dry straw, and prepared for her supper such things as horses love. Jess would neither take food nor rest, but moved uneasily in her stall, and seemed to be waiting for some one that never came. No man knows what a horse or a dog understands and feels, for God hath not given them our speech. If any footstep was heard in the courtyard, she began to neigh, and was always looking round as the door opened. But nothing would tempt her to eat, and in the night-time Drumsheugh heard her crying as if she expected to be taken out for some sudden journey. The Kildrummie veterinary came to see her, and said that nothing could be done when it happened after this fashion with an old horse.

" A've seen it aince afore," he said. "Gin she were a

Ian Maclaren

Christian instead o' a horse, ye micht say she wes dying o' a broken hert."

He recommended that she should be shot to end her misery, but no man could be found in the Glen to do the deed, and Jess relieved them of the trouble. When Drumsheugh went to the stable on Monday morning, a week after Dr. MacLure fell on sleep, Jess was resting at last, but her eyes were open and her face turned to the door.

"She wes a' the wife he hed," said Jamie, as he rejoined the procession, "an' they luved ane anither weel."

The black thread wound itself along the whiteness of the Glen, the coffin first, with his lordship and Drumsheugh behind, and the others as they pleased, but in closer ranks than usual, because the snow on either side was deep, and because this was not as other funerals. They could see the women standing at the door of every house on the hillside, and weeping, for each family had some good reason in forty years to remember MacLure. When Bell Baxter saw Saunders alive, and the coffin of the doctor that saved him on her man's shoulder, she bowed her head on the dyke, and the bairns in the village made such a wail for him they loved that the men nearly disgraced themselves.

"A'm gled we're through that, at ony rate," said Hillocks; "he wes awfu' taen up wi' the bairns, conseederin' he hed nane o' his ain."

There was only one drift on the road between his cottage and the kirkyard, and it had been cut early that morning.

Before daybreak Saunders had roused the lads in the bothy, and they had set to work by the light of lanterns with such good will that, when Drumsheugh came down to engineer a circuit for the funeral, there was a fair passage, with walls of snow twelve feet high on either side.

"Man, Saunders," he said, "this wes a kind thocht, and rael weel dune."

But Saunders' only reply was this:

"Mony a time he's hed tae gang roond; he micht as weel hae an open road for his last traivel."

When the coffin was laid down at the mouth of the grave, the only blackness in the white kirkyard, Tammas Mitchell did the most beautiful thing in all his life. He knelt down and carefully wiped off the snow the wind had blown upon the coffin, and which had covered the name, and when he had done this he disappeared behind the others, so that Drumsheugh could hardly find him to take a cord. For these were the eight that buried Dr. MacLure - Lord Kilspindie at the head as landlord and Drumsheugh at the feet as his friend; the two ministers of the parish came first on the right and left; then Burnbrae and Hillocks of the farmers, and Saunders and Tammas for the plowmen. So the Glen he loved laid him to rest.

When the bedrel had finished his work and the turf had been spread, Lord Kilspindie spoke:

"Friends of Drumtochty, it would not be right that we should part in silence and no man say what is in every heart. We have buried the remains of one that served

Ian Maclaren

this Glen with a devotion that has known no reserve, and a kindliness that never failed, for more than forty years. I have seen many brave men in my day, but no man in the trenches of Sebastopol carried himself more knightly than William MacLure. You will never have heard from his lips what I may tell you to-day, that my father secured for him a valuable post in his younger days, and he preferred to work among his own people; and I wished to do many things for him when he was old, but he would have nothing for himself. He will never be forgotten while one of us lives, and I pray that all doctors everywhere may share his spirit. If it be your pleasure, I shall erect a cross above his grave, and shall ask my old friend and companion Dr. Davidson, your minister, to choose the text to be inscribed."

"We thank you, Lord Kilspindie," said the doctor, "for your presence with us in our sorrow and your tribute to the memory of William MacLure, and I choose this for his text:

"'Greater love hath no man than this, that a man lay down his life for his friends.'"

Milton was, at that time, held in the bonds of a very bitter theology, and his indignation was stirred by this unqualified eulogium.

"No doubt Dr. MacLure hed mony natural virtues, an' he did his wark weel, but it wes a peety he didna mak mair profession o' releegion."

"When William MacLure appears before the Judge, Milton," said Lachlan Campbell, who that day spoke his last words in public, and they were in defence of charity, "He will not be asking him about his professions, for the doctor's judgment hass been ready long ago; and it iss a good judgment, and you and I will be happy men if we get the like of it.

"It iss written in the Gospel, but it iss William MacLure that will not be expecting it."

"What is't, Lachlan?" asked Jamie Soutar, eagerly.

The old man, now very feeble, stood in the middle of the road, and his face, once so hard, was softened into a winsome tenderness.

"'Come, ye blessed of My Father ... I was sick, and ye visited Me.'"